WOMEN IN SOCIETY
A Feminist List edited by
Jo Campling

editorial advisory group

Maria Brenton, *University College, Cardiff*; Phillida Bunckle, *Victoria University, Wellington, New Zealand*; Miriam David, *Polytechnic of the South Bank*; Leonore Davidoff, *University of Essex*; Janet Finch, *University of Lancaster*; Jalna Hanmer, *University of Bradford*; Beverley Kingston, *University of New South Wales, Australia*; Hilary Land, *University of Bristol*; Diana Leonard, *University of London Institute of Education*; Susan Lonsdale, *Polytechnic of the South Bank*; Jean O'Barr, *Duke University, North Carolina, USA*; Arlene Tigar McLaren, *Simon Fraser University, British Columbia, Canada*; Jill Roe, *Macquarie University, Australia*; Hilary Rose, *University of Bradford*; Susan Sellers, *Centre D'Etudes Féminines, Université de Paris*; Pat Thane, *Goldsmiths' College, University of London*; Jane Thompson, *University of Southampton*; Clare Ungerson, *University of Kent at Canterbury*; Judy Walkowitz, *Rutgers University, New Jersey, USA*.

The 1970s and 1980s have seen an explosion of publishing by, about and for women. This new list is designed to make a particular contribution to this process by commissioning and publishing books which consolidate and advance feminist research and debate in key areas in a form suitable for students, academics and researchers but also accessible to a broader general readership.

As far as possible books will adopt an international perspective incorporating comparative material from a range of countries where this is illuminating. Above all they will be interdisciplinary, aiming to put women's studies and feminist discussion firmly on the agenda in subject areas as disparate as law, physical education,

WOMEN IN SOCIETY
A Feminist List edited by
Jo Campling

Published

Sheila Allen and Carol Wolkowitz   **Homeworking: myths and realities**

Jenny Beale   **Women in Ireland: voices of change**

Angela Coyle and Jane Skinner (*editors*)   **Women and Work: positive action for change**

Gillian Dalley   **Ideologies of Caring: rethinking community and collectivism**

Leonore Davidoff and Belinda Westover (*editors*)   **Our Work, Our Lives, Our Words: women's history and women's work**

Diana Gittins   **The Family in Question: changing households and familiar ideologies**

Frances Heidensohn   **Women and Crime**

Ursula King   **Women and Spirituality: voices of protest and promise**

Muthoni Likimani (*Introductory Essay by Jean O'Barr*)   **Passbook Number F.47927: women and Mau Mau in Kenya**

Jo Little, Linda Peake and Pat Richardson (*editors*)   **Women in Cities: gender and the urban environment**

Sharon Macdonald, Pat Holden and Shirley Ardener (*editors*)   **Images of Women in Peace and War: cross-cultural and historical perspectives**

Vicky Randall   **Women and Politics: an international perspective** (2nd edn)

Rosemary Ridd and Helen Callaway (*editors*)   **Caught Up in Conflict: women's responses to political strife**

Patricia Spallone   **Beyond Conception: the new politics of reproduction**

Clare Ungerson (*editor*)   **Women and Social Policy: a reader**

Forthcoming

Eileen Aird and Judy Lown   **Education for Autonomy: processes of change in women's education**

Niam Baker   **Happily Ever After? Women's fiction in post-war Britain**

Jennifer Breen   **Women and Fiction**

Maria Brenton   **Women and Old Age**

Joan Busfield   **Women and Mental Health**

Ruth Carter and Gill Kirkup   **Women in Engineering**

Emily Driver and Audrey Droisen (*editors*)   **Child Sexual Abuse: a feminist perspective**

Lesley Ferris   **Acting Women: images of women in theatre**

Tuula Gordon   **Feminist Mothers**

Frances Gray   **Women and Laughter**

Eileen Green, Diana Woodward and Sandra Hebron   **Women's Leisure, What Leisure?**

Jennifer Hargreaves   **Women and Sport**

Annie Hudson   **Troublesome Girls: adolescence, femininity and the state**

Susan Lonsdale   **Women and Disability**

Mavis Maclean   **Surviving Divorce: women's resources after separation**

Jan Pahl   **Marriage and Money**

Shelley Pennington and Belinda Westover   **A Hidden Workforce: homeworkers in England, 1850–1985**

Lesley Rimmer   **Women's Family Lives: changes and choices**

Susan Sellers   **Language and Sexual Difference: feminist writing in France**

Taking Liberties Collective   **Learning the Hard Way: women's oppression and men's education**

Jane Thompson   **Introducing Women's Studies**

Deborah Valenze   **The Other Victorian Women**

Janet Wolff   **The Art of Women**

Ann Woodhouse   **Sex, Gender and Transvestism**

Women and Work

Positive action for change

Edited by

Angela Coyle
and
Jane Skinner

M

MACMILLAN
EDUCATION

First published 1988

Published by
MACMILLAN EDUCATION LTD
Houndmills, Basingstoke, Hampshire RG21 2XS
and London
Companies and representatives
throughout the world

Typeset by Vine & Gorfin Ltd
Devon, Great Britain

Printed in China

British Library Cataloguing in Publication Data
Women and work: positive action for change.
—(Women in society).
1. Women—Employment—Great Britain
2. Sex discrimination in employment—
Great Britain
I. Coyle, Angela   II. Skinner, Jane
III. Series
331.4′133′0941   HD6135
ISBN 0–333–42129–9 (hardcover)
ISBN 0–333–42130–2 (paperback)

Series Standing Order

If you would like to receive future titles in this series as they are
published, you can make use of our standing order facility. To place a
standing order please contact your bookseller or, in case of difficulty,
write to us at the address below with your name and address and the
name of the series. Please state with which title you wish to begin your
standing order. (If you live outside the United Kingdom we may not
have the rights for your area, in which case we will forward your order
to the publisher concerned.)

Customer Services Department, Macmillan Distribution Ltd,
Houndmills, Basingstoke, Hampshire, RG21 2XS, England.

Contents

List of Tables and Figures

Tables

Figure

Acknowledgements

This book comes out of our work within the Women and Work Programme which we started and developed, with others, at Aston University in 1984. Now the Programme is located at Coventry Polytechnic and is established as a national centre for positive action. Its national and international work includes educational and training development, research, consultancy and advice. The success of our work within the Women and Work Programme is due in no small measure to the number of very creative women who have given and do give time, vision, commitment and sheer sustenance to the Programme's development. This book come out of that contribution and is therefore, as is often the case, the product of many. We would like specifically to thank each of the contributors for their encouragement and support; Jan Jones for all her practical help and Marie Davies for producing the typescript. Finally we want to acknowledge our beloved children who are inevitably 'engaged' in our pattern of work and who, perhaps unknowingly to them, sustain us. In moments of optimism we are glad they have been learning early patterns, choices and consequences each day for women standing 'free'. In moments of pessimism we are sustained by their bright hope and love.

ANGELA COYLE
JANE SKINNER

Notes on the Contributors

Lynn Ashburner has recently completed research on the impact of new technology on gender differentiation and work organisation in building societies. She is now based at the Open University, where she is researching the impact of new technology on managerial work.

Angela Coyle has taught in further and higher education and has written on many aspects of women's employment, including redundancy and unemployment, the subcontracting of employment, training, the labour market and equal opportunities. She has developed a wide range of training courses for women in public and private-sector employment, as well as for women who are unemployed.

Rennie Fritchie has worked throughout Britain, Europe and North America as a management consultant on women's development and training. She has pioneered positive action strategies to increase women's opportunities in paid and other work. She has written (with Jane Skinner) a career life planning guide for women.

Patricia Jones is a management consultant. Her research interests are policy development and implementation. She is currently researching the implementation of equal-opportunities procedures.

Elisabeth Al-Khalifa is a advisory teacher in the field of multi-cultural and anti-racist education. She has undertaken an action research project designed to help school managers to understand and promote equal opportunities in teacher employment and development. She has been consultant to a number of local authority education departments on teachers' development and women's training.

Celia Robinson qualified as a nurse in 1957. After a career break of seventeen years she returned to work first with the NACAB and subsequently for a local authority social services department. She is now Lecturer in Management at the Nuffield Centre for Health Services Studies, Leeds University.

Jane Skinner has held senior management posts in social and community service management, and lectured at Aston University in public-sector management. She has shaped several positive action programmes from ideas into reality including the Women and Work Programme. She co-directed the National Women's Enterprise Development Agency, based in Birmingham and is now an Assistant Director of Birmingham Social Services Department.

Janette Webb studied psychology at Hull and Nottingham Universities, and has worked in a housing insulation co-operative, before doing research at the University of Kent and lecturing in business studies at Aston University and, most recently, Edinburgh University. She has been involved in voluntary groups concerned with women's employment since the 1970s and believes that an autonomous women's movement is central to improvements in women's opportunities.

Introduction

Continuity and change: women in paid work

ANGELA COYLE

This book will be of value to teachers, students, practitioners, individuals and groups who are in their various ways engaged in the project of positive action for women's employment. It is centrally concerned with identifying the processes and structures by which gender segregation and inequality is maintained in the organisation of work and with providing strategies for intervention and change. The book draws upon the considerable activities and research of the Women and Work Programme, now a national centre for positive action in women's employment. It challenges the much believed myth that with formal legislative equality the position of women in the employment structure is 'getting better' – if anything it has got worse.

It is a book about developing strategies. Strategies which will address some of the major problems women continue to face in paid employment. Namely, the overwhelming concentration of women in low-paid, low-status work, which is segregated from men's work and where the real contribution we make is systematically undervalued and marginalised. Our under-representation in positions of power means that we neither participate in nor determine the decision-making processes which so affect our working lives.

The book provides examples of positive action programmes and projects in a number of key sectors for women's employment. However, it does not provide a one-minute guide to positive action nor a comprehensive compilation of trends in women's employment. In documenting some of the changes that have been achieved

1

by 'equal opportunity' measures, it also highlights some of the fundamental limitations of the concept of equal opportunities for women; that is if it does not also challenge other major divisions – of class and race – upon which organisational hierarchies are premised.

We must acknowledge that some of the material of this book relates to white women. Racism runs so deeply into employment practice that black and ethnic minority women are scarcely present in some of the sectors under examination (television, finance and higher education for example) and certainly not within higher paid occupational grades. It is the gaps, the places that positive action interventions have not reached, that seem to us to identify and map continuing tasks. 'Equality' cannot be about getting a few more women into senior jobs, when such gains are made at the expense of others. It is the exploitation and oppression of *all* women which is the challenge to strategies for positive a action.

Our definition of positive action at this point in time is an exploration of structural changes which represent new ways of working, *between* women who have been divided by class and race, *within* work organisations which have been historically premised on white male supremacy. There is no blueprint but the aims are clear enough. To move forward together, in co-operation, in self-determination, to enable ourselves without disabling others.

Women, the new workforce

One of the most far-reaching forces for social and economic change in the United Kingdom over the last three decades has been women's participation in paid employment. By 1986 over nine million women were in employment, representing 44.5 per cent of the total labour force. This now very well documented long term trend (see for example, Martin and Roberts, 1984) began in a period of economic growth from the late 1950s onwards and has continued despite subsequent economic recession. Indeed in the period of deep recession in the UK, 1979–1986, women's representation in the workforce increased by 3 per cent (from 41.4 per cent to 44.5 per cent) whilst, in the same period, men's economic activity rates decreased (from 58.6 per cent to 55.5 per cent of the workforce). Paid employment for women in the UK has become normal for women themselves, their families and their dependants. It makes plain women's important economic contribution to family income. The male as sole family breadwinner is a dying breed; only 18 per cent of households in the UK are now supported by such a male wage earner. The most typical household pattern is that of joint income earners (with 1 in 7 women earning more than their partner) whilst an increasing proportion of women (1 in 4 households) are now the main family breadwinner. It has been estimated that one in three families would be living in poverty were it not for the contribution of women's earned income (Royal Commission on the Distribution of Income and Wealth, 1978).

It was the 1961 Census in the UK which first picked up the growing labour forces participation of women *and* showed that this trend was combined with considerable change in life cycle patterns Throughout the inter-war period and into the early 1950s the predominant pattern amongst women was one of complete withdrawal from the labour force on marriage or at the birth of a first child. By 1961, a change in this pattern was already manifest, with a growing number of women *re-entering* the labour force after a break for childbirth (Hakim, 1979; Myrdal and Klein, 1956). This pattern is clearly reflected in labour force statistics throughout the decades of the 1960s and 1970s, where it was the 35+ age group which mainly contributed to the increased female economic activity rates (EOC, 1982). This distinctive pattern of female economic activity,[1] established over the post-war period is a two-phase pattern of economic activity, of working before and after having children. Dex (1984) has suggested that by the early 1980s women's economic activity had become even more complex, with women having two phases of labour force participation, the 'family formation phase' and the 'final work phase'. During both phases women may have a range of employment profiles including returning to work *between* children. Both Dex and Martin and Roberts (1984) demonstrate that women's quite complex work patterns have come to mean that more and more women are working for longer periods of their adult lives. However the number of women who work *continuously* throughout their working lives (only taking out six months maternity leave before returning to full time work) remains a very small minority which has not increased in twenty years despite the statutory provision of paid maternity leave (Daniel, 1980; Martin and Roberts, 1984, p. 125). Thus although the number of women in

paid employment is almost equal to the number of men, women's
patterns of participation still remain different.

'Women's work': job segregation

It is now very evident that the majority of working women
undertake different jobs from men. The movement of women into
the labour force described here has not been evenly distributed and
for the most part women are concentrated in certain jobs and
certain industries. In part this has reflected patterns of economic
growth. Job growth has occurred in private services (for example, in
finance distribution and retailing) and in public sector services
(health, education, and social services). It is here that female
employment is concentrated. But more than this, women are
concentrated in industries *and* occupations which are predominantly female, with patterns of horizontal and vertical segregation
which, Hakim (1979) has argued, have remained unchanged over a
span of more than eighty years. Horizontally, women are
segregated in low status types of work which are commonly
associated with women. Secretarial and clerical work accounts for
over half of all women's non-manual work, whilst manual services,
especially cleaning and catering, and the 'caring' professions,
teaching, nursing and social work are the other main occupations of
women. Hakim suggests that if horizontal segregation has
diminished slightly since the introduction of the Sex Discrimination
Act (1975), it is because of the movement of men into 'women's
work', rather than the other way round. Vertical segregation on the
other hand, is increasing (Hakim, 1979). Where men and women
are employed in similar occupations men are increasingly to be
found in higher grades. Hakim concludes that women were more
evenly represented in managerial/administrative grades in 1911
than now and 'that it is wrong to believe that the position of women
in the labour force has improved over the century – on the contrary
it has deteriorated quite markedly in some respects' (p. 29).
Segregation within single firms, rather than across sectors, is likely
to be even more complete (see Hunt, 1975). It is more likely to have
increased since the introduction of the Equal Pay Act (1975) as
segregation has been a major employer strategy for evading Equal
Pay. Given that there exist whole areas of work which are

exclusively male or exclusively female, it is hardly surprising that women's and men's perception of their work reflects this reality. Martin and Roberts found that the majority of women regarded their work as 'women's work' (p. 30).

One distinctive feature of women's paid employment which has been key to the development of women as a low paid workforce is women's working hours. By 1986 nearly half of all women in employment were in part-time jobs. Between 1979 and 1986 part-time jobs as a percentage of all jobs increased from 16.9 per cent to 21 per cent and these were almost exclusively occupied by women. The growth of women's employment has been critically linked to the availability of part-time work; those industries where large numbers of women are employed also have the highest incidence of part-time working. When Myrdal and Klein (1956) were making the case for women's right to paid work, they regarded part-time working as the way in which women could reconcile their dual role. Since then part-time work has been identified as a particularly exploitative form of employment (Hurstfield, 1978) and which has been used by employers, not to facilitate childcare needs, but as an effective strategy for creating a cheap, flexible labour force (Beechey and Perkins, 1985).

Predominant patterns of part-time working amongst women can be shown to correspond to patterns of childcare needs. On average women working part-time work 18.5 hours per week, as against an average full-time week of 37.4 hours, and the most common pattern of part-time working is a reduced working day, rather than a reduced number of days per week (Martin and Roberts, 1984, p. 36). Women who have children of school age are most likely to be working a part-time shift that spans the middle of the day (between 10 am and 2 pm) whilst women with children under school age are most likely to be found working an evening or night shift. Martin and Roberts found that 78 per cent of all part-time evening workers were mothers of children under 5 (p. 38). The advantages of part-time working to employers are considerable. On the whole part-time workers are paid less than full-time workers and if employers can keep part-time pay below the weekly National Insurance threshold and below the PAYE income tax threshold then they incur no employers' overheads. If weekly pay levels are kept at a low level by maintaining short part-time hours this also means that many employers are able to evade many obligations under the Employment Protection Legislation (Robinson and Wallace, 1984). Martin and Roberts found that one third of part-timers in their survey did not qualify for benefits or protection (p. 35) and only 9 per cent belonged to an occupational pension (p. 58). If part-time work has helped facilitate women's *entry* into the labour force, it has not enabled any progression within it. Part-time work is overwhelmingly concentrated in low paid, low status work, very few men work part-time and there is very little availability of part-time work in more skilled or responsible work.

Where women work alongside men in full-time non-manual work their pay and conditions of employment are comparable to men's. It is the combination of occupational segregation and part-time working, however, which has enabled women's pay to be determined at levels significantly lower than men's. Many years after the introduction of the Equal Pay Act in the UK women's gross full-time weekly earnings are still only 65 per cent of men's. Poverty caused by low pay is far more likely to be a woman's problem than a man's (Scott, 1984). Nearly 2.5 million women working full-time are low paid. Part-time women workers are even more likely to be low paid. It has been estimated that 92.2 per cent of women in part-time manual jobs and 66.9 per cent of women in part-time non-manual jobs are low paid (Broad, 1986). At the same time all the evidence points to this low paid work being occupied by those in the greatest need; single parents or women whose partners are either unemployed or themselves on very low pay (Broad, 1986).

Universal patterns?

These employment patterns, of job segregation, low pay and low status work are common features of women's employment in European and North American labour markets. Rates of female economic activity in other countries do vary; France, West Germany and the USA are comparable with the UK, although the UK stands out as having the highest rate of part-time work. In Belgium, Denmark and Sweden the rate of female economic activity is lower, with women making up approximately one third of the labour force, whilst Holland and Ireland have the lowest rates in Western Europe (approximately 25 per cent) and with particularly low rates of economic activity amongst married women. Finland on the other hand has the highest rate of full-time female employment in the West and second only to the Soviet Union. In Finland women make up nearly half of the labour force (47 per cent) and this includes a high proportion of mothers with pre-school children (77 per cent). Unlike women in the rest of Europe and US, Finnish women do not have a 'bi-modal' or even interrupted pattern of employment for childbirth, even though there is very little part-time employment (only 16 per cent of Finnish women work part-time) (Kanpinen-Tovopanien *et al.*, 1984, pp. 183–4). It is the Soviet Union, however, which stands out as having the highest rate of economic activity amongst women, with 90 per cent of all women between 16 and 54 in full-time employment. It also has equal representation of women in the labour force, where women make up 51 per cent of the labour force (and 53 per cent of the population).

Some form of gendered job segregation both vertical and horizontal is common throughout Europe and the United States. This is reflected in pay differentials, where women's pay is around two thirds of male rates. Whilst the cultural context of Soviet women's participation in the workforce is probably different from elsewhere, features common with Western economics are very apparent (Attwood and McAndrew, 1984). As a direct result of state action in the 1930s when female quotas were imposed on industrial training schools, women make up a high proportion of technical, engineering, accountancy and medical professionals. However 67 per cent of women engineers are in the lowest grades, with only 1 per cent in the highest. Whilst men make up only 11 per cent of health personnel they occupy 47 per cent of senior posts. In common with Western labour markets women in the Soviet Union are severely under-represented in managerial positions (Attwood and McAndrew, p. 295).

It is tempting to seek a universal 'cause' for these common features of female employment patterns, yet there is no simple explanation for the differentiation of women's employment. Rather, it is clear that the specific form of female economic activity can vary according to cultural and social conditions as well as economic. Gendered job segregation *is* a common feature, but it occurs in different ways in different contexts. What is regarded as 'women's work' in one labour market is not in another. Nor is it always the case that women's occupancy of higher level occupations is necessarily a feature of industrialisation and 'progress'. It is sometimes the case that women are found in senior positions in economies which are less 'developed' and where women represent a small proportion of the total workforce. Only detailed examination of the determinants of occupational *structures* will help to explain the differentiation of women and men's work.

Equal opportunities and positive action

There is now a fairly sizeable body of research that has taken place around women's employment, and which indicates that increased female economic activity has been accompanied by the increased marginalisation and segregation of women in low paid temporary 'women's work'. Whilst it has been projected that the labour force in total will become increasingly 'female', there is nothing intrinsically emancipatory in this trend. The Institute of Manpower Studies, University of Sussex has projected the development of a fundamentally divided workforce, where women make up the bulk of a highly marginalised *peripheral* workforce, whilst a smaller *core* workforce of highly paid, skilled professionals will remain predominantly male.

Since 1975, legislation in the form of the Sex Discrimination Act and the Equal Pay Act, has been in operation which makes the unequal treatment of women and men in employment illegal. Yet the existence of this legislation has made no significant material change to women's lives. Although the Sex Discrimination Act provides the legislative means for overcoming gendered job segregation, not only has job segregation increased since 1975, but there is evidence that the Equal Pay Act has, paradoxically, been a contributory factor in this increase. This has been because the segregation of women's and men's work has been a major strategy used by employers to *avoid* equal pay. Whilst the introduction of the Equal Pay Act did lead to increased pay settlements for women, there was at the same time a spate of men's wage negotiations which sought to compensate the loss of differentials caused by equal pay settlements (Snell, 1979). Legislation, therefore, has not been able to tackle the fundamental problem of women's employment – that is, the segregation and differentiation of women's work. Since the late 1970s women's average pay in relation to men's average pay has dropped back and there are now more women in low paid jobs than ever before (Atkins, 1986, p. 58).

The limitation of the scope of legislation for effecting economic and social change always has to be recognised but the specific limitations of the UK Sex Discrimination legislation is particularly apparent. It has always been very narrowly defined and excludes whole categories of workers and whole areas of discrimination. As Atkins (1986) states: 'The emphasis on *sex* discrimination diverts attention from the real problem of women's second class status. . . . The problem is transformed from one about lack of power into one of barriers to single sex monopolies' (p. 63). It excludes or ineffectively protects part-time workers, homeworkers, pensions, health and caring in the home and it has been left to the EEC Courts and Industrial Tribunals to try to plug many of the gaps (see Hoskyns, 1985).

The other major limitation of UK legislation is the scope for enforcement. Unlike US legislation where it is possible to bring a case on behalf of a group, UK law is premised on individual cases, with the burden of proof on the complainant. Atkins has shown that class/group action in the United States has been much stronger because it is more difficult to trivialise (p. 61) and at the same time supported by much stronger enforcement by US courts (Meehan, 1985). It is not surprising that the number of successful cases brought to the UK courts is small and has been reducing rapidly since the legislation was first introduced (Atkins, 1986; Gregory, 1982). Little redress has actually been achieved through legislation and with the chances of success so small, it is no wonder that few women pursue a case. Some of these weaknesses could be overcome by greater trade union support for equal pay. Snell has indicated that there is a possibility for class action in the UK if equal pay was built into all trade union collective agreements. However, although trade unions have long been committed to equal pay policies there is little evidence of unions incorporating negotiations for equal pay within the collective bargaining process (Gregory 1982; Snell, 1979).

The amendments to the Equal Pay Act (1984) which was forced on the UK government by the European Parliament provided for the first time the possibility of claims for Equal Pay based on equal value. Although this amendment was and is an extraordinarily complex piece of legislation, women seem to take heart from it and there has been an increase in Equal Pay claims based on equal value. At the time of writing a case has been won and a case lost under this 1984 amendment, and it is not at all clear whether it will enable any real gains to be made. Legislation is very much a product of its economic and *political* context. The UK legislation was developed during a period of social consensus and liberal democracy, in which manifest inequality was irreconcilable with meritocratic liberalism, but so was major social change. As Atkins (1986) has argued, the gaps and weaknesses in enforcement are not accidental omissions but integral to the way the law was formulated in the first place – within a framework of pragmatism. What has been left out has 'shackled the effectiveness of the law since its inception' (p. 58) with the enforcement of rights *not* a political priority. UK legislation has always been premised not on enforcement but its 'educative' effect (Atkins, 1968).

The educative effects of sex discrimination legislation is questionable, especially amongst employers. However what in effect has taken place over the last three decades in the UK is the considerable increase in women's participation in the *formal* economy, making inequality and exploitation far more visible. The legislation *does* expose the gap between the ideal and the reality and lessons are being learned fast.

In both the USA and the UK the political onslaught against hard-won rights has made plain that women's rights cannot be pursued in isolation from other civil rights issues. Equality of Opportunity harnesses the concept of change to the existing framework of power. The increase in the qualifying period for protection against dismissal during maternity leave, to two years; the reversal in the Courts of Appeal of an Industrial Tribunal decision awarding equal pay for equal value, and the abolition of the Fair Wages Resolution, all make plain the limitations of the concepts which underpin the law. As Atkins has asserted, the period of sitting tight, doing nothing and leaving it to the law is truly over (p. 67).

The Sex Discrimination Act does allow for interventions in the labour market and employment structure, which seek to overcome ongoing inequality. This action has become known as Positive Action (Affirmative Action in the USA) and an increasing number of local authorities and a small number of private companies have adopted such programmes as an equal opportunities intervention.

(This should be kept in perspective, however, by noting that out of thousands of registered companies in the UK – and this includes local authorities – just over one hundred have an Equal Opportunity Policy Statement.) Measures commonly associated with Positive Action include: an analysis of the workforce; setting goals and targets for the measurement of change; providing a written Equal Opportunity policy statement and the development of specific recruitment, promotion, staffing and training strategies designed to attract and develop identified target groups. Positive action programmes in the UK are on the whole voluntary, not enforced by law, and as yet show little success in the way of measurable organisational change. In the USA, positive action has been underway for longer, underpinned and enforced by contract compliance laws. Robarts *et al.* (1981) cite cases throughout the USA where women's representation in occupational grades where they have previously been under-represented has been much enhanced by positive action programmes. However in the USA too the contradictions are very clear. Whilst more women may have moved into junior management as a result of positive action, senior management grades remain unchanged. *Apparent* improvement can be achieved through the re-categorising of jobs – for example from secretary to administrator – but without any change in either status or pay. Robarts *et al.* also document instances of discriminatory practices which continue to flourish and negate the effects of positive action measures taking place: 'it was discovered some time after the affirmative action programme had begun that the bank was still favouring senior male executives by paying their membership subscriptions to exclusive male-only clubs' (p. 31).

Positive action measures have also been used to maintain privilege. For example, white males in the USA have successfully won court cases against positive action which were designed to overcome the under-representation of women and black minorities (Robarts *et al.* 1981). Positive action may also be negated by other organisational changes taking place, such as economic reorganisation and restructuring – when women may be disproportionately affected by job loss or deteriorating pay and conditions. Nevertheless Positive Action at Work is a developing strategy and one which provides many possibilities for women (see Stamp and Robarts, 1986, for a full discussion).

All the contributors in this collection stress the limitations of such positive action *and* its importance. This is not as paradoxical as it may seem. Positive action, like equal opportunities itself remains harnessed to political, social and economic structures which are built on inequality and divisions. Nevertheless what positive action has achieved is to shift the focus away from individual women (and their supposed shortcomings) and onto a more organisational, structural perspective. As Coote and Campbell (1982) have argued: 'It shifts the focus of the campaign for equality towards a recognition of the system which sustains male supremacy and suggests that men themselves must actively participate in the process of change' (p. 131).

Experience and practice

Now as we look hard and critically at 'equality of opportunity', it becomes plainer that what women need is not to be 'equal' with men in any simple sense but to build employment practices which are informed equally by women's experience. Whilst every woman has her own highly individualised biography, there are recurring, universal, common experiences amongst women which challenge much of the theory and practice of management, work organisation and organisational behaviour. Even studies of women's employment have tended to focus on women's experience of work in relation to their childcare and family responsibilities, and thus ignored the very concrete structures and very real social relations which keep women 'in place' in the employment structure (see Feldberg and Glenn, 1984, for a full discussion; Cockburn, 1983a, for a study that goes a long way to redress this research 'blindspot').

There are aspects of women's experience which have already helped to redefine the position of women in employment. The myth of the male breadwinner no longer holds up to critical examination. Women's mounting protest against sexual harassment at work makes plain some men's attempt to maintain control of women in the workplace. There remain many more mythologies to challenge. The idea that men are a totally committed workforce whilst women are not has no material evidence to support it yet as Laws (1976) has stated 'the heroic male professional . . . characterised by his zeal for his work' is the standard against which women are measured (p. 36) and against it women come up deficient: 'The myth of female motivational deficit has much in common with the deficient theories of black personality which in the sixties "accounted for" the "inferior" motivation and attainment of black Americans' (Laws, 1976, p. 37).

Women's experiences also challenged much that is commonly understood about the nature of work. Each chapter in this collection is focused on a specific sector of employment and as well as 'explaining' the subordinate position of women in employment hierarchies, many also make clear that hierarchies do not reflect the distribution of skill and talent in the way that they are presumed to do. There is an important distinction to be made between management – as those who hold managerial positions – and management as a series of key functions. The two are not necessarily the same. Women indeed occupy key functions which are vital to the running of organisations but it is clear that the holding of managerial positions still depends on masculinity as being a desirable (if not essential) qualification. Women are not the only ones to expose this situation and the 'new managerialism' (see for example, Peters and Waterman, 1984) has opposed the idea of organisations having a unity of interests steered by a single focus of power, decision-making and competence at the top. However the alliance ends there, for as Landry *et al.* (1985) intimate, the 'new' management is still 'full of groomed testosterone and that curious blend of machismo and zen' (p. 57).

Women are unpicking and challenging male power, male ways of working and some of the myths of managerialism. This book is concerned with looking at patterns of women's employment in the context of different forms of work organisation. Each chapter is focused on a specific sector of employment and develops explanations for the now very familiar position of women in paid employment, within a concrete examination of organisational structures, relationships and ideology. Authors have identified some of the ways in which the relationships and expectations of women and men are formalised in organisational structures and processes, which continue to set the parameters of women's participation in paid work. The picture built up is not an optimistic one, but it does break down the totality of women's subordination in paid work into what is in fact a multiplicity of practices and relationships. In this identification of the daily lived experiences of women, there is indeed hope for individual and collective action.

Perhaps the most fundamental challenge, however, that now has to be made to the concept of equality of opportunity is the implicit goal for women to achieve equal representation with men in a context of competition. What can never be made explicit is that only some can 'win'. Equal opportunities does not challenge the divisions between women and men and between women. Equality for some women cannot be achieved in isolation or at the cost of others' civil rights.

There are real differences in the experiences and situation of women according to class and race. Working-class women, perhaps without formal educational qualifications, are most likely to occupy low-waged jobs. Black minority women in particular have higher rates of unemployment, are most concentrated in the lowest-paid, least-attractive jobs and have the least access to training. Racism in the labour market locks black women in particular into a highly marginalised workforce and yet one which, arguably, has been critical to the development of vital industries and services (Bryan *et al*. 1985). Positive action which does not recognise and constructively address the divisions between women, created by class and race conflict cannot provide the basis for alliances between women based on *common* as well as differing experiences.

Every chapter in this book makes plain the *limits* of equal opportunities if it is not accompanied by organisational change. Most women in paid employment are in positions within organisational hierarchies where there simply are *no* opportunities for promotion. Our understanding of gendered job segregation will probably go no further without the continued examination of male practice; without a better understanding of the process of gender and of femininity and masculinity, without a better understanding of the issues between black and white women and the effects of racism which can drive a wedge between us. This is not a book of answers but is does provide an account of some beginnings. Beginnings which are fraught with divisions and contradictions but where women have begun to intervene in the structures of organisational hierarchies, where women are finding a voice and becoming agents for change.

Note

1. Patterns of female economic activity have varied according to class with evidence that working class women have always been more likely to work (Black, 1983; Jephcott, 1962).

1

Who cares? Women at work in social services

**JANE SKINNER and
CELIA ROBINSON**

Introduction

From Octavia Hill to Dame Eileen Younghusband, from 'the
almoner' and the 'child care officer' to the 'social worker' and the
'home help' – the great names and the key roles in the world of
personal social services are associated with women. Yet in these
social services a growing number of men have come to work within
such services including within voluntary and community organisations. This trend is particularly evident in managerial positions
throughout the social services. It could be said that since the
introduction of equal opportunities women constitute a small and
perhaps declining percentage in the management of such services.
The basic grade jobs, and particularly those with virtually no career
prospects such as home helps, remain the almost exclusive province
of women.

This chapter sets out some dimensions of these trends, attempts
an account of their emergence and moves to an analysis which
considers why developments in social services' staffing have
followed this particular pattern. In the light of this we then set out
some positive action approaches to reverse the marginalising
of women at work in these caring services. Some such actions
we have been involved in through the Women and Work
Programme, whilst others are feasible – but have not yet been
tried out in practice.

The context – roots of/routes to the 1980s in the social services

The 'personal' social services are often called the fifth arm of the 'welfare' state. They comprise a range of practical support, advice and supervisory 'control' services for a variety of vulnerable groups. Often these groups are referred to as 'client groups': key ones include 'at risk' children and families, those with mental or physical handicaps, mentally ill people not in hospital and 'frail' elderly people. The personal social services – usually called simply the social services, if not 'The Welfare' – are mainly organised and managed by local authority social services departments. Over 90 per cent of public spending on social services is by these departments, the remainder being through voluntary organisations. The scale of these is small compared to the health and education services; around 2 per cent of all public expenditure is devoted to them.

Nonetheless these social services departments are large-scale organisations with annual expenditures running into millions of pounds. As with most other care and control services a large portion of this money is spent on the staff who deliver, manage and administer the services. Each social services department has a wide range of jobs at the 'care face', manual and professional, residentially based and in the community. Most of these basic jobs, *whatever* their type, are performed by women. Examples of typical 'departmental staffing profiles' are as follows: a county department in a middle-sized authority has 2326 salaried staff (out of 4640 total employees) with 1644 women and 682 men. In another county department women comprise 79 per cent of employees and men 21 per cent (results of postal survey 1986).[1]

Obviously proportions vary somewhat from department to department, but overall women form a majority of employees, the proportion usually being over 65 per cent of total staffing. Their jobs vary from home helps to care assistants and day centre staff to the key professional social worker posts. At the point of delivery, social service jobs have been and remain largely womens' work.

The profession of social work is at the heart of modern social services organised in large local authority social services departments. It is the defining profession in social services; most managers in departments are drawn from the social worker ranks. Indeed the importance of their professional qualification, the Certificate of Qualification in Social Work (CQSW), extends to departmental directors who normally hold this social work qualification.

Historically, social services departments came into being in late 1971 as a result of reforming legislation recommended by an official committee of enquiry chaired by Lord Seebohm (Seebohm, 1968). This committee looked at the work and effectiveness of small departments which had 'delivered' personal services since 1948 – the children's departments, the welfare departments and the mental welfare section of public health departments. It found these small departments were not meeting social service needs satisfactorily. Key problems identified included under-funding of services, gaps between services and overlap of provision in some cases. The 1968 Report also identified the lack of management, research and development as a handicap to effective working. Seebohm recommended the formulation of unified social services departments capable of promoting services for all client groups, able to fight for resources within local authorities and providing, by their size, an attractive career structure for 'able' staff. In November 1971 these unified 'one door' social service departments came into being, each with a director of social services who would head up the second largest department in each local authority. The new departments typically had and still retain a management structure with director, deputy director, assistant directors and principal officers being responsible for overall management and planning. Middle managers at 'area' or 'specialist' functional levels carry out day-to-day management. In the transition from small scale to large scale, from two tiers of management to four or five tiers in the 'chain of command', the position of women in managing social services worsened at a stroke!

Up until 1971 social work and its management had been largely a female sphere with the partial exception of the old welfare officers, who were often ex-poor law officers. The first social workers, employed by organisations like the Charity Organisation Society, were women who did the job at least partially out of a 'volunteer' ethic. A resilient influence from these origins was that such jobs were 'seen' as not necessarily needing 'pay and promotion' to ensure effective work. The bureaucratic traditions of the poor law administration are also part of the 'roots' of modern social services (Payne, 1979). These 'voluntary' and 'bureaucratic' roots are both real foundations of the current social services. But it was the pre-1971 children's departments who employed most qualified social workers. Over one third of all the 'directors' of these departments – children's officers – were women and the 'voluntary' ethic of service remained very strong. As Eve Brook and Ann Davis (1985) cite, Home Office figures (1970) show 77 of 174 children's officers to have been female. This should have meant that 30 to 40 of the new social services directorships would be filled by women. This is particularly so since ex-children's officers figured very prominently in the 1971 appointments. In fact only 14 of the new directors were women. Such data as is available from individual departments about the overall pattern of senior management appointments in 1971, indicates a similar pattern of female marginalisation at deputy, assistant director and even principal officer levels.

Years after the implementation of Seebohm's recommendation in 1971, which created the multi-tiered social services departments, it is an open question whether bigger has meant better in terms of service efficiency or quality of service planning and management. It has certainly enhanced career advancement possibilities for those who step on to the social services management career ladder. From 1971 onwards this has been in majority men; as Brook and Davis (1985) state: 'The statistics available on staffing in the personal social services show clearly that as one moves away from the front line of welfare one leaves behind the territory of women and enters the territory of men'. The very act of stressing the importance of management by Seebohm has led to women being marginalised as managers in the new big departments.

The unification of small agencies into the social services certainly heralded the arrival of 'management' with a belief in the managerial ethic to ensure good planning and delivery of effective, efficient services. This 'managerialism', much in favour during the expansionist times of the early 1970s throughout the public sector, seemed to mean that men were seen as having the qualities to direct and plan the new social services. Perhaps this was linked to then current notions that such qualities should include bargaining power, large scale planning skills, dynamism and 'leadership skills'. The Seebohm Report states this about the new directors widely in services:

> *He* will have to weld groups of workers differing widely in training, professional outlook and tradition into a team with common objectives. *He* must be able to *command the confidence* of members, to persuade them to provide more resources for the services, to maintain a reasonable balance between the demands

made on behalf of different groups in the population, and at the same time *to stand up* for the department (our emphases) (Seebohm, 1968).

Managerial qualities seem to have been defined in masculine terminology and it is not therefore surprising that mainly men became the new directors. It was a historical turning point. Women had become exceptional and very much a minority as social services managers. Women were thus also ushered out as significant policy advisors and public figures in these services.

At the time of writing the picture 'at the top' has changed little; there were 95 male directors of social services and 10 women in such posts. We wrote to all social services departments in England and Wales asking them to identify where women were in management posts. The 41 responses received show a remarkably consistent picture at top management levels but more variations in middle management. In almost one third of departments which replied there are no women working in the top three tiers of management, whilst the remainder rarely have more than two females at this level. (Figures from some departments were incomplete as currently only a proportion regularly keep gender-based statistics in respect of particular job categories such as the various levels of management.) Only at the lowest tier of management posts are women near to 'equality' with men in numbers. For example, in one department of 186 manager posts in residential and day care establishments, 86 were held by women. Yet even this contrasts with, or rather 'inverts', the gender percentages for those in the basic grade jobs. In one London department 65 of the 84 social workers are women yet only 33 of the 59 senior social workers are female. These trends are mirrored in other 'traditionally' female strongholds as recent research into both nursing and teaching management indicates. Davies and Rosser (1985) and Elisabeth Al-Khalifa (Chapter 4) identify remarkably similar patterns to the one we have just set out. Why has the entry of men into the council services led quite rapidly to their disappropriate representation in all management grades and their almost complete domination of senior management?

Reasons for the male majority in care management

At the most fundamental level, assumptions and beliefs about gender and self-definition can be seen as creating concrete problems for women at work in any other than 'support' roles. This is notably so for women and in management roles. The existence of deep-seated assumptions about men and women's different orientation to work are now well documented in numerous studies (see Feldberg and Glenn, 1984, for a full discussion). This not only means that organisations may overlook women when considering staff for promotion but that women themselves are constrained by what is deemed to be appropriate behaviour and aspiration in women. If it is assumed that it is only men who are job-orientated, then for women to seem so construes them as 'behaving like a man'. It is this conflict which contains women in their lower status support roles, rather than their lack of ability or aspiration.

Yet a work environment dominated by men is alien to women, perhaps particularly in social care organisations whose professional and grassroots workforce is, as we have said, mainly female. Male values are now enshrined in the 'social care' workplace – for example through the subordination of the workforce to a 'multiplicity of superiors' in many tiers of management (Chandler, 1986). This can lead to a stifling of the characters of both male and female members of the workforce with a consequent lack of honesty *or* freedom of expression. Social workers are faced with the same dilemma in their interactions with clients where the inappropriate use of their authority may lead to a breakdown in the very trust which is needed to achieve improved social functioning. Women in zero power positions in male-dominated organisations are in a similar position to the clients expected to contribute to the development of an effective relationship with a social worker who is perceived as an agent of social control.

Organisationally, a number of processes wittingly or unwittingly serve to reinforce the position of women as 'outsiders inside' the agency. These range from the most important, and most recurrent, informal daily interactions between women and men working together – to formal procedures and policies. In day-to-day working, male values about what is appropriate behaviour to demonstrate, for example, competence and career promotion 'potential' will tend to informally rule. Even progressively-inclined male promoters only begin to recognise and then, perhaps, question their unconscious marginalising of women when, for the first time, they consider in a training context their routine behaviour as supervisors and staff developers. This means that the daily reality of male dominance in informal and formal meetings with eye contacts, referencing and opinion setting, is rarely seen as other than natural. It is usually not even self-recognised. Socialisation, expectation and behaviour form a vicious but comfortable circle which can reinforce the continuance of women 'knowing' their place at work.

Such attitudes and behaviour patterns are consistently reinforced by the organisation, the family and society as a whole. Much of the evidence for this is illustrated by the experience of women part-time workers. Most part-time workers in social services departments, are women – home helps, care assistants, social work assistants, typists and domestic staff. It is less common for professional or managerial staff in social services departments, to work on a part-time or a job-share basis because of their limited availability during conventional working hours.

Recruitment of female part-time workers in such high numbers and in a wide range of low grade posts is a strong manifestation of the extent to which the organisation believes women want part-time work. Society believes women want to combine part-time work with family care; women accept both the guilt and the role. Yet a part-time launderer in an elderly persons home has been an able and respected member of a group set up to identify training needs for all the staff in such homes. She recognises her own potential but these abilities have come as a surprise to more senior male managers. The initiative to enrich her role as a member of a working group preparing an induction training manual came from her female manager. This long established pattern of part-time employment in local government has the appearance of a throwback to the 1960s; at which time manufacturing industries were actively recruiting women as unskilled, low-paid workers by advertising 'school hours' shifts. Local government also has an interest in recruiting a low-cost labour force. Women may be cheap to employ either because they fill part-time posts or because they are professionally unqualified. It may also not be coincidental that in social services departments many of these staff are home helps, social work assistants, care assistants, all of whom work primarily with the elderly.

An interesting manifestation of equal opportunities policies in local authorities is the recent emergence of job-share schemes. Indications are that these posts are more often sought by women. Job-share posts also share a number of common features with part-time posts causing similar career blocks. For example, a significant barrier to career development is the limited nature of the training available to those not engaged in full-time work. Much of the training provided is in-house, home-grown and offering no qualifying certificate which might be regarded as marketable elsewhere. In our experience it is rare for full-time professional qualifying training (CQSW) to be offered to those working part-time. The assumption made is that part-time workers generally work a sufficient number of hours to enable them to undertake the Certificate in Social Services (CSS). This is a three year job related sandwich course validated by the Council for Education and Training in Social Work (CETSW). A minimum of fifteen hours weekly is required to be spent in the work place in addition to the two days given to training. Managers may not agree to release staff if this reduces their hours at the work place and the manpower budget may be insufficiently flexible to allow for an extension of hours. This situation leaves women workers locked into part-time, low paid and often manual jobs.

Thus daily realities feed into the processes of choice leading to, or not, attempting to attempt a career progression through promotion. A particularly significant reinforcer of women's rarity in management is the way in which those with management 'potential' are identified and thus how aspirations are built, dampened or strangled after conception. It may also be that many women feel quite detached from the possibility of advancement and indeed may be alienated from it as they view existing models of management undesirable and not for them.

These 'internal' barriers amongst women are real but should not be viewed as meaning an absence of ambition. This attitude may well constitute a wholly positive response at the individual level to current organisational facts and one which sustains self respect by avoiding involvement in what may be seen as demeaning or damaging kind of work. It may also be a practical detachment from what is undoubtedly a 'stiffer' competition for women than for men.

However, this is not the whole picture. Many women *do* envisage the possibility and the desirability for themselves of moving up the ladder. As the excellent research work of Davies and Rosser (1985) indicates, 'career orientated' women in the National Health Service may have to possess twice the relevant experience and qualifications of their male counterparts – in order to move onto the next rung of the career ladder. More limited evidence we have from social services departments indicates a similar pattern of discrimination. Women it seems are expected to work at the 'careface' but not manage caring work.

Planning to change women's place in social services

So the barriers and the detachment are not wholly or even mainly amongst women. There is a 'supply' of careerist women who face undue difficulties in gaining promotion. We have outlined two major contributory factors. The first – imagery surrounding 'competence' in relation to managerial work and the second – the processes by which people do or do not get to the 'start line' of being in the competition for promotion.

Where systematic staff development and appraisal are absent, incomplete or subtly sexist the process of imaging and identifying 'potential' will probably be in terms of likeness to existing role models and behaviours amongst those who are already managers. These images are heavily skewed in the masculine direction. In addition, the cut-back situation in the public sector has led to increased weighting being given to personal qualities like 'toughness', 'decisiveness' and 'dynamism'. There is an obvious danger that those seen as possessing such qualities will not be females! More recent trends, at least in the literature of management (see for example, Moss Kanter, 1984; Peters and Waterman, 1982, 1984), point up that managerial qualities needed for excellent organisations include such attributes as creativity, 'leadership from among' and sensitivity to others. This would seem likely to help managerial roles and women to be seen as compatible! It remains to be seen if existing organisational processes – enable such linkages to work through into pre-selection, selection and promotion decisions within social services agencies.

Currently it is common for pre-selection processes unwittingly to favour men to 'go for' the first rung of the ladder. The 'hands up' approach to starting to move upwards remains common and this tends to favour men. Much research on self images and competency and potential indicates that males, from boyhood onwards, tend somewhat to 'over-rate' their objective capacity and competence. Thus they may 'over' aspire for the next step up. The converse is true for girls and women. Some have called the latter the 'Cinderella Complex' and we would suggest the former as the 'Handsome Prince Complex'! Whilst the 'hands up' situation remains, specific career development training for women in organisations and other ways of encouraging females to go forward (such as mentoring and self-development groups) are needed to help create a better balance in the pool of candidates. Similar careful selection is needed to assure a balance in those who gain sponsored management training or who are selected to work on difficult career developmental assignments or to 'act up' temporarily in management roles. If not those seen as most likely to succeed are likely to be 'likely lads'!

In social services, as in other parts of the public sector, inability to respond to pressure for change has contributed to the perpetuation of 'conventional' employment and promotion patterns. Such organisational rigidities can be attributed to a number of underlying causes. Firstly, the bureaucratic and administrative nature of social services departments inhibits flexibility and a sensitive, rapid response to changed in the environment because of the over-riding dependence of the organisation upon procedural form and accuracy. This approach is supported by a management style which reacts to events occurring within the given framework of existing systems and procedures. A more proactive management style would enable the development of policies and strategies to facilitate change for the benefit of women and other different employees. Secondly, the prevailing system's approach to management found in many social services departments at best facilitates structural and procedural changes related to organisational design and format. The approach fails to foster the centrality of human resources and potential. Thirdly, social services departments have some of their roots in the historical conservative tradition of 'welfare' which has seen women as 'servants' and not 'masters'. Women employees may consequently be perceived by male managers as service providers and not service managers. The culture of the organisation is pervaded by male values. Chandler (1986) argues that the hierarchical structure, with its in-built notion of superiors and inferiors or subordinates is 'character warping' for women, stifling freedom of expression and the creative use of intellect. Finally, local government conservatism tends to assume that the existing way of doing things is satisfactory (East Sussex Consultancy and Training Agency, 1985).

If the day-to-day realities, as well as prevailing organisational behaviours, for women in social services do not provide cause for hope and the barriers to change multi-faceted, we nonetheless do not subscribe to the inevitability of negative trends continuing. We will therefore suggest a range of possible positive actions to bring about both a better balance in the staffing of various levels within social services delivery and management as well as an improvement in what management constitutes in these services. We will focus – in this consideration of taking positive action – particularly on those initiatives with which we have been involved.

Taking positive action for change in social services[2] Taking positive action may itself be seen as controversial. Our view is that it is necessary and desirable if unfair discrimination, past and present, is to be stopped. It is worth noting that departmental managers tend to regard the imbalance in the position of women and men in their organisations as inevitable or natural. Alternatively, some believe that there may have been prejudices and barriers in the past but now all opportunities are open to the progress of women within social services: so that what happens now will be a matter of unfettered personal choice. A comment from one director of social services is illustrative of this attitude: 'Quite frankly the sex of any applicant for a management post is not a factor which receives consideration but there are certain categories for which women would not consider themselves reasonable applicants.'

Yet the reality for most women working in social services agencies is that there are extra barriers and career blocks continue to present almost insurmountable obstacles to progress. Indeed, women increasingly seem to be getting trapped by part-time work, ineligibility to apply for professional qualifying training and they are not seconded for any significant training. Career breaks, which are more commonly taken by women in local government, slow down prospects of promotion by reducing relevant work experience. Continued recruitment into traditional female jobs (clerical and typing), with limited or no career progression opportunities beyond that of supervisor, again continue to affect women's opportunity to gain the necessary work experience which would equip them for higher posts.

In the beginning to take positive action any agency has a number of choices and it may be helpful to see these in a continuum of strategies as set out in Table 1.1. The agent introducing change strategies may be external to the organisation or part of it. Of course, often the change agent grouping comprises a mix of 'outsiders' and 'insiders'. The Women and Work Programme has frequently been an external prime mover, raising the possibility of taking positive action to equalise work opportunities for women. In the public sector generally, particularly within urban local authorities, the elected council as a political force may have made the choice to adopt an active approach, beyond the equal opportunities policy statement, to changing the imbalance in their staffing. Indeed, in response to our letter asking departments throughout England and Wales of their plans to ensure equal opportunities for women staff, almost half the metropolitan districts and London boroughs were working in the context of a formal equal opportunities policy. This varied in its extensiveness and *only four* departments in our sample had a comprehensive policy encompassing a range of strategies from training and 'regulation' to developmental work.

Table 1.1   *Positive action strategies and changing opportunities for women in social services*

Strategy	Main focus of strategy
Training of women for higher status work	Individual change
Training of women and men re attitudes and practices	
Development of personnel policies process and practices	
Organisation development Experiments in work roles/processes	
Changes in structures and management approaches	Organisational change

It is important to be aware of the trigger factors, or from where the impetus for change is emanating. 'Top down' change approaches, sometimes only occurring because of external pressure, risk *not* taking into account the views and daily realities of women at work at the bottom of the organisation. 'Bottom up' change approaches, often initiated by committed individuals or small groups of female staff, risk being 'contained' by those in authority – either completely, by the legitimacy of the case for change being denied, or partially, by positive action strategies being defined wholly in terms of the need for individual change 'down amongst the women'. We suggest that an effective strategy should be a mix of approaches to bring more women into the higher echelons of the organisation *and* to effect changes in the way in which management is conducted so that female behaviours are valued. Thus strategies would aim to bring about both individual change *and* changes in organisational processes, particularly the ways in which work is managed and thus what constitutes valued management behaviour.

Currently, most of the initiatives we know about risk being partial. Strategies, where they exist at all, tend to be focused on achieving individual change without any challenge to the *modus operandi* of the organisation at work. In each initiative with which we have been, or are involved, we seek to, at least, *raise* the importance of such process and culture changes occurring in the organisation if movement is to be beyond the individual level.

In an initiative we helped effect within a large metropolitan social services department there were two principal trigger factors. The first was organisational: the department had undergone a reorganisation of its management structure and this made starkly clear that there were tiny numbers of women in senior management in the agency. It also meant there was a broad readiness to consider new initiatives in management development and training. The second was more particular. Within the personnel and training section of the department was a member of staff whose commitment to promoting equal opportunities actively was considerable. This meant that both the early discussions between the Women and Work Programme and the agency occurred in most constructive context with energy focused on *how* to make a training-based initiative happen rather than negotiating about its appropriateness.

The training section, with its active staff members, studied the department's gender-based statistics and this highlighted several points in the organisational structure where women became 'stuck' or 'blocked' in career patterns. These were as follows. The lowest graded clerical posts were female-dominated yet the higher clerical administrative grades showed near sex 'balance'. Thus the first block was in the area of progression from routine clerical to higher clerical work. The second blockage was identified at the 'entry into management' point. Whilst women comprise a majority in almost every service-delivery post, including those of social worker, they were in a minority at the first level of management – the team leader or other supervisory post. As this is the first rung of the management career ladder, this situation was agreed to be of crucial importance in reinforcing the continuance of female under-representation in management generally. The third sticking point was found to be at entry into top management. Whilst some 20 per cent of middle management posts were occupied by women, they were virtually non-existent in the top three tiers of management – the key policy formulating positions.

In the early discussions we agreed that all three sticking points should be addressed in a strategy for lasting change but that the pilot training project should focus on one of the three points of blockage. We quickly moved to agreement on action in the second area. This was for three major reasons. First, we all considered this to be the crucial area if seeking to bring about long-term, as well as short-term, changes in the composition of management in the agency. (Only those who step onto the first rung can climb higher.) Secondly, there was an ample number or pool of women in the top service-delivery grades to draw from for a pilot programme on a single agency basis. Thirdly, the two other identified road-blocks on women's career paths were to a limited extent beginning to be addressed in other ways. For clerical staff some positive action training was being developed and run within the department itself. So it was negotiated and agreed by the agency's management to conduct a pilot training-based project aimed at the entry-into-management barrier. The pilot project had twin aims which were to: enhance *promotion prospects* of women employees (particularly senior 'delivery' level staff) in the Agency, and raise awareness of the problems and issues women face amongst those responsible for promotional employment practices in the department.

In the light of these twin aims we decided upon a three-part programme which would provide for separate training for 'promoters' (that is managers), and 'promotees' (that is women staff), with a final joint workshop to explore issues of common concern. The three-day course for 'promotees' provided assertion training and an orientation to management. Promoters – female and male – explored issues of equal opportunities as well as personal and organisation attitudes to women as managers over a two-day period.

For this pilot programme nominees were self-selected for both parts of the course. The response from potential promotees was surprising and overwhelming, considering the organisation's lack of consciousness about the development of its female workforce. Indeed, worry had been expressed by senior management that there would be insufficient interest in the programme as women appeared to be '*most* happy' in their work situations. Nominations were more than double the number which could be accommodated on the course and this was with very little publicity about the course within the agency. This surge of interest served to challenge the myth in the organisation that women were less interested in management than their male colleagues. There was less demand from promoters; more female than male managers were interested in attending this course. Whilst this was disappointing, it was not unexpected!

Those on the 'promotees' course were especially appreciative of an all women's group. Initially, the apparent quietness of the group concerned tutors. When this was checked out with them, the women thought their quietness reflected the lack of competitive elements which they felt was an inevitable feature of mixed training courses. They found the absence of male involvement a liberating experience which gave them the opportunity to explore issues of common concern to women. One of these was orientation to management. The women saw the prevailing male management style as competitive, aggressive, political and individualistically orientated. Managers were interested in pursuing outcomes which were to the benefit of their careers but which failed either to ensure effective service delivery or to utilise the skills of the female workforce effectively. The prevailing culture of management, unconscious though it might be, has a negative effect on female employees, often causing them to become demotivated in terms of aspirations for promotion. It is a model of management which can be seen by some women as inevitable and as excluding alternative styles which could be developed by women managers. This had led some participants to decide to opt out of considering entering management. This was discussed in some depth during the course with the benefits and costs of 'joining' in order to change explored by the participants and tutors. The possibilities of managing in a way which was not alien to themselves as women were explored.

'Promoters' also self-selected for training and thus the choice to attend indicated a commitment to the ideals of equal promotion opportunities for men and women. Working in single sex groups on the first day male promoters were, nonetheless, surprised at the extent of their own discriminatory practices towards women promotees. They began to recognise the limitations of male models of management, though all found it difficult to move beyond reacting against the limits of the 'old' modus operandi to trying out – for example – more collaborative, inclusive decision-making and work planning.

It cannot pass without comment that black women were not represented in any of these courses. For them there was the added dimension of a hostile white environment. There were few black managers to serve as role models for aspiring black females in the department. Their absence in this programme led to a fresh training initiative for black women employed in this Department.

In the evaluation of the course conducted by both groups there was unanimous agreement amongst 'promotees' that it had proved successful and, for most, was also an entirely new experience in a training setting. The course had helped the women to reorient themselves, as well as to assess their own abilities and skills together with building confidence. It had introduced some approaches to self-presentation, negotiating at work and had considered conventional approaches and practical alternative strategies towards managing people and processes. This pilot group very strongly expressed the view that further similar courses be run for others within the department who wanted to attend the courses but had not been allocated a place. The format of each course, tutored by two trainers from the Women and Work Programme, was also considered effective. It was based on exercises and discussions interspersed with short structured inputs. The promoters' course was also judged by participants as valuable. Both they and the tutors considered two days to be too short a time, especially on a non-residential basis, to both raise awareness and develop some practical ways forward in equal opportunity staff development and selection approaches. We feel the recognition, particularly amongst male managers of their usually unwittingly 'over-sight' of female staff, requires at least two course days and, then at least, an equivalent period needs devoting to developing some approaches, primarily to non-discriminatory management. The joint workshop for promotees and promoters was also found to be too short at half a day. The intention was to explore ways of progressing forward together. This was discussed – with nearly everyone considering that higher priority should be given by the agency to taking positive action and to lessen gender-based discrimination. Of course, after this short training programme a number of unresolved 'issues' remained. Also, the 'dawning awareness' which several participants felt needed further pursuing in single sex groups. It is heartening that a number of the promotees formed a network as a result of the course – partly in order further to explore and develop approaches towards 'managing' which more closely reflect their own core values.

Although there was an understanding that this initiative was training-focused and small-scale, we envisaged this pilot programme as the beginning of a strategy to equalise opportunities; to lessen neglect of women's talents and values in this agency's practices. Thus, after the pilot programme was completed we presented a report on the pilot courses and some suggestions for further interactions to the agency's management team when it met later that year. In essence, our suggestions were to build on the pilot programmes, especially in view of the known demand for such courses; to organise further courses to address this crucial career 'block' for women at the entry into management point. We further suggested that the Women and Work Programme help 'root' this kind of training into the agency by an approach which trained a group of in-house trainers so that after a second course, the department could conduct subsequent programmes itself. But beyond this we strongly suggested that a broader approach needed setting in motion with its main framework being sanctioned by top management. To help start this we urged that a senior management seminar be held to work through and set out a framework for taking positive action, this to include work 'beyond' training – in areas such as personnel practices or experimenting with new organisational approaches to women and men working together. These options for a forward strategy have been quite positively received at a meeting with the department's management team. So far in practice, however, the agency continued in its established ways giving little priority to equalising opportunities for its women staff and perhaps rationalising this by pointing to its very active training-based strategy to change racial attitudes and the 'white' composition of staffing. We consider that achieving racial and sexual equal treatment often go hand in hand. Both deserve definite positive action if an organisation wishes to effect changes in the discriminatory status quo. There are, however, some differences: women are present in large numbers in social services agencies, albeit concentrated at the bottom, whilst black people are largely not in the employ of such organisations. So some different action priorities emerge – as well as many common ones – if movement to achieve a more balanced staff structure of women and men *and* of black and white people is to occur.

We have set out a consideration of this initiative in some detail as it illustrates both the potentials and some of the pitfalls of training-based approaches as ways to change organisations' staff 'profiles' and their practices. On the positive side our monitoring of participants in the course, particularly promotees, indicates that the course was effective in building confidence and widening career choices. On the other hand, the pilot programme has *not* so far become rooted in the organisation's normal in-service training schemes. We do not believe that short foci on the 'equal opportunities' aspect of general management courses constitutes a viable substitute – though *this is* occurring and will have some value. The extent to which organisational practices and processes, from the day-to-day interactions to policy statements, are moved as a result of such inputs on general courses, is hard to establish in any direct sense. However, we observe little in the way of general management interest in attempting small-scale change. A management strategy to lessen the imbalance in staffing within the agency is as yet still to be elaborated. It is all too easy for experimental training-based initiatives to bite the dust in the 'dynamic conservative' climate of many public sector organisations. However, the seeds of change have been planted and we believe that the effects of several individuals empowered by the training courses will make some positive movement *at least* in parts of the organisation and also eventually affect changes in policy.

A different approach to positive action initiatives has been developed in a county's social services department, where the 'prime mover' was a female middle manager who used the 'assignment' opportunity provided by a management course to research the position of women in the agency setting. This was in the context of her local authority's new formal policy of being an equal opportunities employer. She then helped develop interest in her findings through informal talks with top managers of the agency. As a consequence of this a departmental working group was established, chaired by the deputy director (male), to suggest strategies for creating equal opportunities for women and men in the department. The working party comprised its chairman, two people from the personnel and training section of the department, four representatives of service management, together with one person from the county's personnel section. The group held two meetings and appeared to have focused very quickly on two specific aspects of eliminating discriminatory practices. The first area was distribution of information about the county's equal opportunities policy and the second, recruitment practices, particularly interview techniques.

At this stage we were called in to provide 'outside' expertise. Having been well briefed, with background papers by the 'prime mover' who was a member of the working party, we decided to open up questions amongst working party members concerning this rather 'defensive' focus. There *are*, of course, excellent reasons for ensuring that interviewers in an authority know they are not permitted to discriminate against women – particularly when interviewing. But compliance without management commitment to equal opportunity policies brings about little in the way of different decisions either before, or during or after key selection decisions. Even in the USA, with its different culture and considerably stronger equal opportunities legislation, women still have – on average – less than two thirds of men's average pay, and progress to, at any rate, top management remains slight. Whilst ensuring no one says the offensive question can be an important first step, we suggested this policy advisory group worked through the possibilities of attempting to bring some attitude and behaviour change amongst managers. In this way compliance might move towards commitment to equalising opportunities at work for women in the agency. This strategy included some departure from 'normal' expert behaviour. After some genuflection to convention at the working party meeting (that is, establishing expertise and experience), we gave a short input on the various definitions of equal opportunities. Then the group was asked to work for a short while, at first individually and then in pairs. They were asked to set out where they perceived their department to be, in reality, in terms of managers' attitudes towards equalising opportunities for female staff and what they, as key managers in the department, felt should be the situation. After this work we moved to discussion of a range of strategies which could be attempted to make forward movements from the status quo. (The current agency profile is very typical with professional service delivery being female-dominated and management male-dominated.) After working in this way, the 'correct' interview approach was seen by most as *part* of a process of changing attitudes, probably best comprising one section of management development courses which would also tackle attitudes and staff development approaches. We explored training for promoters, for women staff and for teams working together. The working party agreed with the logic of attempting 'experiments' in new ways of working together – starting with teams where willingness to be innovative existed. The importance of involving 'typical' women staff in detailed elaboration of approaches to equalise opportunities was also acknowledged. At the point of writing the working party has just reported – and they have broadened out their considerations. So the possibility of a creative, experimental approach to attitude and behaviour change within the agency does now exist.

We have also been involved in a range of other advice and training initiatives which have direct relevance to the social services. Senior managers from social services departments have participated in the Women and Work Programme's Executive Development Programmes. We anticipate that these women will break through the 'glass ceiling' into posts at departmental director or assistant director level. We have been called on to give advice to a number of social services agencies concerning approaches to improving opportunities for female staff and we welcome such first steps. However, we are also very conscious, from the many connections we have and contacts made with us by a range of women within the social services 'industry', that it remains the exceptional employer who is taking any positive action.

A framework for action

If the constraints and barriers outlined in the previous section are to be overcome fundamental changes need to be made to the way social services departments are managed. So far it seems political, managerial, personnel and training initiatives lack the coherence and breadth needed really to implement equal opportunities.

Policies or statements of intent are made without reference to their impact in relation to other policies with which they may conflict. For example, internal recruitment policies inhibit the achievement of equal opportunities in the department because these policies block the access of external applicants to posts. Likewise, policies relating to financial cuts and closures without redundancy limit career progressive prospects for those not made jobless.

There is a preoccupation with bureaucracy and organisational structure. The solution to a malfunction is usually seen in terms of structural change. More thought needs to be given to the motivation and effective use of human resources. Approaches need to be developed which take into account engaging rather than overlooking the talents and qualities of female staff, especially in managerial work.

It is to be hoped that social services management will become more aware of gender issues and recognise the value of women and men working truly as colleagues. Women need to be given a fair chance to move from the 'care face' to the higher levels of managerial and planning work.

Positive action policies are needed to redress current imbalances. The limited initiatives which are occurring in social services departments should be expanded and extended beyond training or formal policy statements. Job sharing enables women and men to meet their personal and family commitments without the limitations to career prospects imposed by part time working. Job rotation offers broader experience, and consideration should be given to the enrichment of jobs by offering greater variety and more responsibility. Changes can be made to disciplinary procedures to discourage sexual harassment at work. Training initiatives should be developed to heighten awareness and encourage behavioural change. Recruitment should be aimed at positively attracting women to apply for managment posts. This should be supported by internal training programmes to equip women for posts in management. Less conventionally, networks of women workers should be allowed to develop and opportunities given for such support groups to meet. Service delivery issues which affect women should be addressed by women in social work, perhaps in working parties reporting to the departmental management group. Professional qualifying training courses should address gender issues both as they affect social workers and with reference to service delivery. None of these measures are particularly radical and in themselves they will not be successful unless they are actively supported and implemented by management.

Every agency about which we know has gross imbalances in staffing both in gender and race terms. The 'masculinisation' of the caring services appears to be the norm. We consider this inequitable and likely to prove a mistake in efficiency and effectiveness terms, as well as for those many women who are 'neglected resources' in their departments. We consider it a shared responsibility for women and men employed in social services committees to change this. We think it likely that women will continue to be those who will be the agents for change often battling against conventions and risking ridicule at every turn. We have no ready-made recipe for a quick and easy change. But we know from experience of the last years as trainers and women who are/have been managers, that *significant* and *positive* change can occur when two or three prime movers set out to achieve movement – even against the odds. We leave to those who believe the current situation to be equitable and efficient lengthy explanations of the problems associated with generating change. We shall continue to engender, encourage and assist taking positive action within the organisations for social care and development in our society.

Notes

1. Information from a postal survey of males/females in posts in London Authority departments of social services conducted in Summer 1986 by one of the authors.
2. Many of these comments draw from pilot training and development programmes for social services departments developed and conducted by ourselves in the Women and Work Programme between 1984 and 1986.

2

Policy and praxis: local government, a case for treatment

PATRICIA JONES

Introduction

> Women's committees in the face of so much to put right, in the
> face of Councils . . . beset by inertia . . . are going to need their
> best instincts to survive (Cunningham, 1986)

In a mature democracy the persistence of gender inequality ought to
be the concern of all political parties. In Britain it is women in the
Labour Party who are in the forefront of putting equal opportunities
(EO) for women onto political agendas. Adverse publicity in the
press, particularly that focusing upon the activities of the late
Greater London Council's Women's Committee has created an
illusion of radical activity wherever a local authority women's
committee exists. There is a great divide between the illusion and
the local authority realities. This is not surprising – local authority
organisations have to be taken as we find them; power, authority
status and policy-making resides with those who are white and
predominantly male. It is through this structure that EO policy
objectives have to be implemented. It also comes as no surprise that
the potential for blocking formal initiatives is high. Consequently
progress towards policy implementation in those authorities that
have adopted EO policies is varied. Equal opportunities as a

concept is concerned with both the behaviour and the values of individuals within organisations and the orientation of the organisation itself. It is in theory an all-embracing and complex philosophy. As the philosophy becomes grounded in organisational realities, it appears that EO becomes almost exclusively the concern of those who feel discriminated against.

Within local authority organisations that have a formal commitment to ameliorating gender inequality a range of strategies have been devised to address the EO issue. These may consist of statements concerning equal access (no formal race or sex bar) through to positive action which acknowledges that active organisational strategies must be pursued if women are to advance their careers within hierarchies. In particular, into those areas where women are traditionally under-represented, most notably formal management positions. A positive change in the orientation of a local authority organisation (that is, towards a lessening of overt and covert discrimination) implies the integration of the concept of EO into every area of local authority activity. Ultimately the policy should become obsolete, as local authorities and individuals within local government incorporate anti-discriminatory practice as part of a normal way of working. Public sector job advertisements announce the fact that a number of local authorities have EO policy statements, but precisely what does this mean?

This chapter seeks to combine a 'bird's eye' view of EO policy formulation with a 'worm's eye' view of the process of EO policy implementation. It begins by outlining a political route to EO policy formulation and raises some of the issues that surround 'top down' EO policy directives. The second part of the chapter focuses more specifically upon a range of interventions that are moving local authorities towards either formalising EO policy statements or implementing and developing existing EO policy objectives. It is not the intention here to condemn or praise specific local authorities, whatever stage they are at along the 'EO road'. This chapter represents a confluence of views, opinions and experiences of women currently working at different levels, in different departments within local authorities that have EO policies and those that at present do not have formal policy statements. The information gathered while researching this area was given freely and in confidence by local authority employees. This has led to the decision not to name individuals. Local authorities will be identified only in cases where information has been reported in the press or published elsewhere.

Addressing equal opportunities at the level of the organisation

Political decisions taken at the elected member level to devise and support EO policies is the 'top down' starting point for many local authorities. The adoption of an EO statement heralds the intention of an authority as an employer to examine its own organisation. The aim is to eliminate obvious structural bias by developing anti-discriminatory practices as a means of achieving equality of opportunity for employees and potential employees. This is one way of bringing EO to the attention of local authority bureaucracies. There are others, most notably emanating from departmental managers. The new managerialism, with its emphasis on efficiency and effectiveness, leaner organisations and the pursuit of excellence, has led to a re-examination of staff development policies within local authorities generally. Almost by default an examination of the under-utilisation of existing employees has focused attention upon women, who constitute the largest single group of local government employees. This trend in management and how it works in favour of women is discussed later in the chapter. For an examination of how EO is developing generally within local authority social services departments and education departments see chapters 1 and 4.

An outline of a not untypical political route to 'getting EO issues' formally acknowledged and ratified at the elected member level can be depicted thus. A case is put forward by active female Labour councillors and local female Labour Party members that the local authority both as an employer and as a provider of services is failing to address the needs of women. The case may be based on specific collected evidence and informed by the experiences of women in other local authorities. A broad policy statement is formulated to address the perceived issue of discrimination. The 'issue' becomes the sole concern of women and to a lesser extent male councillors who have been elected on a pro EO platform. Periodic interest is shown both for and against the policy by elected members and the local media, particularly during the run up to local elections. A committee of elected members may be formed to look more closely at the issue. In order for policy strategies to be developed, the committee needs servicing with research data. For this purpose a women's unit may be set up and may take on a number of functions, (i) to aggregate the views and experiences of women in the community vis à vis local authority services, and (ii) to examine the ways in which local authority policies and departmental practices and procedures discriminate against women. Organisational legitimacy may be gained by locating a unit under the umbrella of a servicing department, such as a chief executive's office or a policy and resources unit. The women's unit may or may not have a budget.

The development of anti-discriminatory practices and the achievement of EO policy objectives may ultimately become the responsibility of a sub-unit of a local authority department. Officers appointed to work in the unit may be recruited from within the authority but more usually they are appointed from outside the organisation. The unit feeds reports and recommendations to a women's committee who in turn make recommendations to other departmental committees. These recommendations may influence the practices and procedures of departments.

In 1982, the year in which women's committees were becoming a political reality in a number of Labour controlled authorities (Webster, 1983), only 18 per cent of local councillors in England and Wales were women. Of this small percentage, it can reasonably be estimated that not all female councillors will give active support to equal opportunities gender issues. In spite of their small numbers the impact women councillors have had upon local political systems appears great. However the apparent gains made in terms of policy interventions at the expressedly political level can be transitory. A change in the political complexion of a local authority may signal the demise of women's committees and womens units. Ironically the obverse also holds, that is, that the existence of political will in itself is no guarantee that an EO policy will be wholly or partially implemented. It does not take a change in political control to rend asunder or dilute EO policies. The political world is so volatile and reputations can be made or lost by association with innovative policies. The Labour controlled local authority of Glasgow is a case in point. In 1986 it chose to ignore its party's policy on lesbian and gay rights. This active omission is no different in outcome to the result of actions taken by Rugby local authority. In 1984 on becoming Conservative controlled the authority removed clauses in its policy that sought to end discrimination on the grounds of 'sexual orientation'. The examples clearly demonstrate that discriminatory practices fuelled by individual prejudices cut across party political boundaries. At any given point in time, 'parts' of an EO policy may be 'dispensed' with, especially during the run-up to local elections. Which Labour-controlled authority, looking for an additional term of office, would dare to be seen to be using public money to support 'reservoirs of venereal disease' (the term used by Lord Halsbury to describe homosexuals in a House of Lords debate in 1986)?

The hallmark of a progressive local authority may be the existence of an EO policy statement. Equally such a statement may condemn an authority to the ranks of the 'Loony left'. In any event, a high-profile and innovative EO policy that aims to tackle sex discrimination may be devised never to be implemented (Button, 1984). Such a policy may instead serve other purposes, for example, to 'buy off' those groups who accuse the authority of operating discriminatory practices, or to form part of a public image an authority may wish to foster in an attempt to demonstrate its accountability to a major section of its community. Some commentators argue that until large enough numbers of women hold status and power positions in organisations, we will have no impact upon political systems (Lovenduski, 1986). If this line of argument is pursued, then at present within formal political and local authority organisation structures women are powerless to prevent the production of token policies. Given the very small percentage of female councillors who are actively nudging local authorities in the direction of making EO policy statements, or implementing EO policies by reforming existing policies and practices, the existence of women's committees must be viewed as a success. For those women councillors who spend many hours battling in committee rooms for incremental shifts in departmental policies towards the attainment of EO policy objectives, the existence of women's committees are in themselves no guarantee that EO policy implementation is realisable. Obviously EO is a controversial issue, but policy statements emanating from those authorities who are formally concerned with addressing the issue of gender discrimination appear to be mere iterations of political common sense. Take, for example, two components of policy statements from two local authorities. The first addresses women as consumers or local authority services, the second the local authority as an employer:

> to consider the position of women in relation to all council services and to strengthen links between the council and the community, with a view to ensuring that the interests of women are properly served by the council.

> to ensure that no job applicant or employee receives less favourable treatment on grounds of sex, disability, marital status, sexual orientation, responsibility for dependents, age, trade union or other political activities, religious beliefs, spent offences or is disadvantaged by any conditions or requirements which cannot be shown to be justified.

Once an EO statement is adopted by a local authority, its responsibility for implementation rests with management. A policy is only a general statement of intent, but when it is clearly defined in terms of specific objectives, targets and goals, it can become a device for improving control and accountability within an organisation. If aspects of an EO policy are precisely specified (the 'what', the 'how' and the 'when' of target setting), and if senior managers support the aims of the policy, departments and ultimately the local authority should (in theory) achieve EO policy objectives. The most tangible parts of an EO policy usually constitute 'action areas' and are now well known. They include an examination of conditions of service, recruitment and selection procedures, training and staff development. The intention appears to be to make local authority structures 'woman friendly'. Most typically the case for change rests on accumulated evidence of how existing local authority practices and procedures discriminate in favour of white men by ignoring the needs of female employees (see for example Local Government Operations Research Unit, LGORU, 1982).

A report by the Women's Adviser in the London Borough of Greenwich draws attention to what is fundamental to any implementation process: those departments which have set out most clearly their equal opportunities objectives have achieved the most significant changes.' For these departments there was over a period of two years a 13.5 per cent average increase in the number of women at SO2–scale 5 level. Clearly inroads can be made into the altering of the gender clustering within the present local authority employment pyramid – women at the bottom, men at the top, (London Borough of Greenwich, 1986). If the implementation of an EO policy is approached in the way that the implementation of other local authorities is approached – 'here are the departmental targets, go forth and achieve them' – then gains will be made. For the many individuals treading the EO path the specification of targets and goals is a very necessary first step on the road to implementation. However it cannot be taken for granted that clarification of EO policy goals is underpinned by a clear understanding of why an EO policy is required in the first place.

The existence of EO policies engender at one and the same time apathy and hostility, heated argument but little real debate, deadly combinations to be confronted by those responsible for implementing equal opportunities. Managers (predominantly male) may be forgiven for being bewildered by statements issuing forth from EO policy-makers, containing as they do a veritable shopping list of those whom the authority wishes to serve more adequately. Such pronouncements can be anathema to those individuals who have 'fought' their way up through the bureaucracy to attain positions of power, authority and responsibility. Those who sincerely believe that they do not discriminate against women. Those who admit to choosing the best man for the job even if it is a woman. It is these individuals who are affronted by the assumptions of their 'political masters' that they do discriminate in favour of white men. The 'commonsense' inherent in EO policies is after all part and parcel of their good management practice. Observations by an EO officer (women) illuminates this grey and sensitive area of managerial discretion:

> An over-riding philosophy of the local authority is that management are eternally correct, this is a male management view of themselves. Some of our initiatives, for instance the designing of new job application forms, implicitly and overtly cast aspertions on and criticise management. For I guess essentially our initiatives can be viewed as a taking away of the responsibility of individuals to act in non oppressive (non sexist and non racist) ways. Perhaps they fear losing power. One has actually said, 'what makes you think we can't do this job because we're not half female?'

The case for equal opportunities has to be made continually, it has to be 'sold' to individuals even though formal EO policy statements have brought to the fore sex discrimination as a legitimate organisational concern, as behaviour to be guarded against. The same officer outlined a response to one of the initiatives her authority was pursuing in an attempt to make the organisation 'woman friendly':

'We are not a benevolent society so why should we act out of step?' This came up when we sought to increase maternity provision. The initiative was viewed as an unjustifiable luxury. Of course the underlying assumption is that women shouldn't be at work if special concessions have to be made for them.

These examples partially explain why EO policy initiatives may come to grief. Quite simply, it is because they challenge the 'fairness' of the status quo, and the values and belief systems of those who benefit from the present system remaining unchanged. Complacency and not conspiracy appears to be responsible for EO policy initiatives not having their expected impact. One Midlands authority has had an EO policy in existence for ten years, and a recent internal document on policy progress stated that 'it is firmly acknowledged that continuing discrimination creates barriers which prevent individual women from realising their potential'. A London borough that has had a Women's Committee for more than three years reported that the structure of their employment pyramid was a cause for concern:

women are over-represented in the lower grades with 94.8 per cent of all women on SO2 level or below. Worst still, the largest proportion of women on these grades are concentrated on scales 1–3. Whilst the numbers of women and men employed by the Council are almost equal, women make up under 1 per cent of all officers on the council above PO5.

At the point at which the impact of EO policies is discernable, at the level of headcounting, local authorities are generally admitting that there has been little significant change in the numbers of women 'moving up' hierarchies. For those authorities in which the issue of sex discrimination is a legitimate formal organisational concern, attention needs to be turned towards the development of policy goals that seek to create a climate of awareness in which formal EO initiatives may come to fruition. It is no easy task to grapple with the complexities of organisational cultures, to pin down precisely what constitutes the 'grey area' of organisational behaviour, the environments of individual departments and units, the points at which policy objectives flounder. However it is easy to become overwhelmed by the enormity of the task of changing the organisation's culture. A measure of comfort may be drawn from, as one policy analyst argues, the view that radical organisational change may be the culmination of a rapid succession of very small changes (Lindblom, 1965, 1979). It was stated at the beginning of the chapter that equal opportunities is concerned with the behaviours and attitudes of individual men and women. Women are included here because we become socialised into work environments and exhibit discriminatory behaviours towards our own sex by directly and indirectly supporting the dominant white male organisational culture. It is as much the responsibility of individuals to change organisational cultures as it is the role of management to issue formal directives about ways of working in line with EO policy objectives. If it is the intention to bring about change, the 'people element' in organisations may be ignored at the policy-makers' peril.

Discrimination is all-pervasive and (unfortunately for those seeking to ameliorate it) does not reside in just one part of a local authority, where it can be readily identified and 'picked off' (Johnson, 1984). Equal opportunities policies are thus of necessity ambitious. The actual policy statements themselves could however be made much more succinct if each authority adopted as a guiding principle the statement 'we will not discriminate in favour of white, middle-class males'. In any event the adoption of EO policies by a small but growing number of local authorities has enabled inequalities to be exposed. There now exists some data on the position of women workers in local authorities. Whether or not women are in manual or non-manual jobs, the overwhelming majority of local authority female employees are concentrated in low-grade, low-status, low-paid jobs with little, if any, prospect of advancement. Numerically women continue to dominate in the traditional areas of female employment within local authorities (education, social services and libraries), but are still grossly under-represented in the management structure of these services. Women who hold non-manual jobs generally occupy servicing roles (for example, clerical, secretarial and administrative posts) firmly placed at the bottom of the organisational pyramid. Reductions in local authority spending and the contraction of services has meant that a significant number of women are and will be losing jobs due to staff cuts and the privatisation of services. Women's paid employment (which can be taken generally to mean the jobs men do not and will not do) disappears, only to be absorbed by women who of necessity take on the roles of unpaid carers, or low-paid employees of the private companies to which local authority services have been contracted out (see Coyle, 1986; Webster, 1985).

Downward trends in public sector spending have an impact upon local authority organisational environments, uncertainty and job insecurity breed an atmosphere of intense competition. It is within this context that EO policies are being announced. This need not mean that such policies are doomed to failure. For there is little evidence to show that during times of relative prosperity and near full employment institutionalised discrimination is 'lessened' or that the sexist and racist attitudes of individual employees evaporate. But it is not all plain sailing, even when agreed EO policy action areas are being pursued. A female Labour councillor was informed by one of her colleagues that it would be 'unwise' for her to be seen supporting recommendations put up to the women's committee by the women's unit. The councillor left the committee meeting before a vote was taken. The blatant exercise of power and influence at the elected member level sets the general tone of local authority organisational environments. The bureaucracy functions by individuals anticipating and complying with the wishes and decisions of central power sources. Senior officers usually know 'who is whose man' in political circles. Such an awareness may ensure that individuals do not 'hitch their wagons to falling stars'. As long as the 'stars' who are fixed or on the ascendant do not 'drop' an EO policy, then no matter how conceptually ill-equipped officers may be, no matter how much floundering goes on around putting the policy into practice, the EO line will be toed. As an officer from a West Midlands authority put it, 'the EO issue is taking off, it isn't popular, but individuals realise they must front up to it if they want promotion.

One of the dangers with top down policies is that people may go through the motions of implementation, without paying adequate attention to the nuts and bolts of policies, the small steps that need to be taken to achieve policy targets. Equality of opportunity may be on political agendas but in order for policies to achieve a level of departmental priority they must be sold to those in formal positions of power and authority. Similarly individuals for whom the policy is for (everyone who is not white, able-bodied and male) must also have EO policies sold to them. This pincer approach will help to create an environment in which policies come to have meaning. One way of achieving an unfreezing of the climate in which inertia flourishes is through taking positive action. Positive action strategies need to be put into operation before equality of opportunity can be achieved. Such action programmes enable women both to overcome barriers in work and to challenge the undervaluing of the work they do (LGORU, 1982, 1984). It is perhaps prudent here to point to the important difference between positive action and positive discrimination. Briefly, positive discrimination concerns discriminating in favour of women and may result in allegations of reverse discrimination, the red herring often used to deny the legitimacy of positive action strategies. Whereas the case for taking positive action (acting in favour of women) rests on the widely-accepted premise that women are disadvantaged. Women and the work they do are undervalued in local authority employment structures (Johnson, 1984). These structures reflect the occupational segregation of the labour market, which is based on traditional assumptions governing the division of labour into men's jobs and women's jobs. This sexual division of labour has generally resulted in the ghettoisation of women into unskilled low-paid work.

Two broad issues emerge from an analysis of local authorities that have EO policies: the first is that unless EO policy objectives are broken down into feasible targets and goals, and until individuals in bureaucracies are held accountable for goal and target achievement, EO policies are doomed to fizzle out during the implementation process. The second point to emerge is that attention must now be directed towards progressing beyond statements made on job advertisements. Attempts must be made to create an environment in which equality of opportunity becomes a reality for individuals. As the status quo discriminates in favour of white men, and is geared towards their needs, positive steps must be taken in the first instance to redress this imbalance, by ensuring that women are better represented at all management levels. In fact women employees themselves have to be made aware of the reasons why their employer has an EO policy and how such a policy may enable them to take positive decisions in genuine choice situations. This is not a one-way street, it is in the interests of local authorities to efficiently utilise existing female members of staff, the latent talent on the pay roll (see LGORU, 1984). It is perhaps a truism to state that it takes a very long time indeed to bring about real change within local authorities. 'Innovative' policies are aspirations and may remain as such until they are grounded in reality. In one Midlands local authority a considerable amount of time has been spent by female officers in convincing chief officers that an EO statement is not the same thing as an EO policy!

Equal opportunities and the individual

At Wolverhampton, the local authority has a policy of awareness training for staff involved in the selection and recruitment process. An officer felt the initiative to be double-edged: 'we are running the risk of enabling individuals to become more refined in the ways they are racist and sexist, but I guess we have to start somewhere.' One commentator has suggested that precisely because sex discrimination is on political agendas, men have found alternative strategies to maintain their dominant position. They have done this, it is argued, by developing intricate sets of more subtle sexist behaviours (Sargent, 1981). There is no substantive research evidence to suggest that male officers in local authorities spend a significant proportion of their time devising ever more subtle sexist strategies to foist on unsuspecting female colleagues. Sadly the development of sexist strategies need not be laboured over, for normal work environments, comprised as they are of unconscious discriminatory behaviours and the use of individual discretion grounded in unquestioned 'commonsense' assumptions, produce practices that are fair in form but unfair in their impact. Women themselves subscribe to male meritocratic visions, and some feel it necessary to justify promotion by denying their sex, 'I got this job because I'm very good . . . not because I'm a woman.' Some even add, 'if I can do it so can others.' This attitude concerns a misconception about positive action, that is that women's achievements will be belittled and undervalued purely because the organisation has a positive action programme. There are very few women in senior management positions within local authorities (a generous estimate would put the figure at 1 per cent), thus fears that an incompetent army of women riding on the wave of positive action are about to flood the top end of local authority hierarchies is a premature concern. But such views reinforce widely held unquestioned sexist assumptions. Day-to-day interactions within departments can provide a window onto the world of indirect discrimination. A woman chatting over coffee with male colleagues discusses a woman in another office: 'it must be really difficult for her to leave such young children . . .'. This remark adds to the commonly held notions of 'divided female loyalties'; the mother, all mothers, are marked out as people who cannot give one hundred per cent effort to their job.

Casual conversations pass into the collective unconscious of offices, units, departments and contribute to the creation of an environment in which indirect discrimination can thrive. Is it any wonder that women are under-represented in management hierarchies? Within the competitive hierarchies that characterise local authority organisations, women by dint of being party to the perpetuation of male value systems are all too often 'persuaded' that they neither need nor deserve to achieve formal status positions. Indirect discrimination, the use of management discretion, is difficult to challenge. Six local government officers shared an open plan office. The unit was under pressure from elected members. One of the officers was a woman, and on one particular day (and over a private matter) she burst into tears while at her desk. This incident had a disproportionate effect upon her male colleagues. After much rumination they came to the conclusion that 'this job is too tough for a woman'. The incident was recounted by one of the male officers who was 'very concerned about placing women in such stressful jobs'. The point of this anecdote is that the woman had no idea that her male colleagues viewed her behaviour in this way, and that she had been judged and had been found wanting, not only as an individual, but the whole of womankind. In a following round of appointments a man was recruited to the unit, because he was the 'best person' for the job.

Perhaps the most subtle sexist strategy now prevalent in local authority organisations is one adopted by those who have some knowledge of EO gender issues. These individuals support EO as being a 'fine idea', the rider being, 'as long as it doesn't cost a lot'. The status quo is guarded by those who know what not to say and where not to say it. Senior managers can demonstrate to all that they are addressing EO policy issues by, for example, creating EO officer posts within their departments. One such post holder stated that over a period of twelve months she had researched and collated views, opinions and statistics on the position of women in the department, but in the whole of her twelve months in post, not one departmental manager had formally consulted her on any EO policy issue. The bolt-on approach to securing policy implementation through the creation of new posts and structures has obvious limitations. An EO officer may become the 'someone who deals with that sort of thing'. Thus sex discrimination as an EO policy issue can become marginalised and runs the risk of being viewed as tangential to proper departmental business.

For those committed to EO policy implementation confronting widespread and ever present apathy is a soul-destroying business. However the existence of apathy has presented some individuals with the chance to introduce small changes: 'On the whole, management are so disinterested they give EO officers a great deal of autonomy. With the support of councillors, changes do slip through and are implemented before they can be blocked.' (Equal Opportunities Officer).

The use of administrative discretion can work both for as well as against policy implementation. But organisational legitimacy is vital, if a 'change programme' is to have any impact. Such a programme must be co-ordinated and integrated authority-wide and be managed from the 'top'. To be anything other than token gestures, formal initiatives must ultimately gain the acknowledgement and support of top management. The existence of a formal policy can enable individuals to challenge discriminatory practices and behaviours. (Though, it is a brave woman who brings a case of direct or indirect discrimination against her employer.) Ironically woman-focused initiatives can result in women feeling that they have been unfairly singled out because they are not effective in their jobs. For those senior managers who are proactive in pursuing either formal EO policy objectives, or cost-effective human resource management strategies, it can come as a surprise to find that their initiatives are treated with much suspicion. 'I don't know why I'm on this training programme. I was sent by my line manager.'

It is difficult to present with any degree of accuracy an overview of EO policy progress in those authorities that have formal policies. Certainly the views and opinions of women who work in local authorities (with or without formal policies) are remarkably similar; blocked career paths, sexual harassment and draconian mangement practices are cited time and again. However, as an outsider looking in, it appears that there is a qualitative difference in organisational environments between those authorities that have a formal policy and those that do not. *This difference can be linked almost exclusively to legitimacy.* In the absence of a formal policy, EO type initiatives have to be low key and introduced almost through the back door; individual women place themselves (and their careers) in precarious positions by teetering on the edge of what the organisation defines as legitimate activity. Those who are concerned with EO policy implementation are gaining a new sophistication and are now well versed in local authority organisational realities. As one EO officer expressed it, 'notification of training programmes for women is not sent out through the usual channels because of gate keepers; women get enough of a ribbing for going on courses anyway.'

It is all too easy to dwell on barriers and blocks to EO policy implementation. The inescapable fact is that a chapter such as this can only be written because some local authorities, as major employers of women, have set sail in whatever fashion into uncharted waters. It is these authorities who have taken the first steps towards acknowledging that sexist and racist behaviours exist within their organisations. The existence of a policy is an important yardstick against which individuals can measure progress. It can also provide a framework within which 'legitimate' demands can be made upon the organisation. People (women as well as men) have to become aware that it is in their interests to make an EO policy 'work'. While the conscious and unconscious exercise of management discretion may delay implementation, the converse is also true. The use of management discretion can effectively promote equality of opportunity for women within local authority organisations. While a small number of women in less than half the local authorities in England and Wales have been successful in placing sex discrimination onto formal political agendas, there are far more women in many more authorities who have sexism and racism as felt and perceived issues on their own personal agendas.

Acting positively

The development of a personal politics is one way of achieving good anti-discriminatory practice, the change in individual attitudes and behaviours that forms the substance of successful EO policy implementation. It is ultimately a way of being, and can become for some women a lifetime's battle to struggle against discrimination. In terms of personal integrity, for many women there is no choice. Choices, however, can be made concerning the ways in which personal agenda items may be translated into strategies for pursuing EO policy objectives. Through the use of management discretion women in formal status positions may act as mentors to other women. This way of using management discretion has made and continues to make an impact upon the promotion and development of women in organisations. This strategy is not dependent upon the existence of a formal EO policy. This raises an important point about positive action strategies at the informal level: all too often such strategies take place in a vacuum and affect only very small numbers of women. While the attitudes and values of women in status positions may contribute to the creation of a climate of awareness in which overt and covert discrimination can be lessened (whether it be at office, unit or department level), when these key women cease to be active, gains made are in danger of disappearing. Mentoring is an important activity in so far as it can improve the quality of working life for some women. However, it is most effective when it is part of a wider organisational development strategy.

Those responsible for implementing EO policies within local government – elected members, chief officers, personnel and training officers, members of women's committees and trade unions – have a large task ahead (see LGORU, 1984). There are however a number of strategies that can be adopted to help push equal opportunities forward within local authorities. But it is important at the outset for implementers to have a clear idea exactly why equal opportunities is an important issue, before they can sell policy initiatives effectively to management and to other employees. There are a number of issues that have to be untangled if initiatives are not to become piecemeal and ultimately ineffective.

Knowledge and awareness

It appears that implementers in a large number of authorities spend a goodly proportion of their time accruing data on the position of women in their organisation. Using statistics (gender-based) can strengthen the case for pursuing certain initiatives, but given that equal opportunities is being pursued in generally hostile environments, the collection of data may become an end in itself. In order to create a climate of awareness amongst female employees local authorities institute training and development programmes. Such programmes are visible signs that an authority is seriously pursuing an EO policy. On the surface this may appear to be a straightforward approach to policy development. However, if training is not to become an end in itself certain basic design issues need to be addressed.

(a) should training programmes be compulsory?
(b) should priority be given to single-sex training programmes (for example, woman-focused personal effectiveness programmes)?
(c) should training programmes be for all women irrespective of grade or department?
(d) should training programmes be offered only to certain grades of women across departments?
(e) should training programmes be offered to women from all grades in one department?

Some other questions that may be raised are: how long is a training initiative a pilot initiative? What is the likelihood of a successful training initiative becoming part of mainstream training programmes?

Within local authorities implementers usually interact; in fact, one individual may wear a number of different hats. What follows is an example of how one individual woman combined a number of different roles to translate personal agenda items into a strategy that was 'sold' to senior management. This particular local authority had a formal policy statement but no specified policy objectives. A female personnel officer was aware of the stagnation at certain grades across the authority. Women particularly appeared to fare less well than men in internal promotions. On the whole, women appeared less likely to put themselves forward for promotion or for in-house training programmes. The personnel officer was also chair of her union's EO committee. The committee agreed that the authority ought seriously to be pursuing policies that sought to enable women to overcome blocks and barriers to career advancement. In her role as chair, she wrote a letter to her boss stating that the union membership were formally requesting that the authority run training programmes for women in line with the programmes currently being run in other authorities that also had an EO policy statement. She did not personally sign the letter. On receiving it her boss passed it to her to deal with; resources were tight, but some money could be made available for a pilot programme. An external agency was brought in. To ensure that sufficient women took up the training opportunity a 'pincer' approach was adopted: departmental managers were invited to sponsor women for the programme and at the same time letters were sent out to individual women inviting them to take up the training opportunity. Before the closing date had arrived the programme was 50 per cent oversubscribed. An evaluation of participants three months after the programme had run (evaluation by participants and line managers) found that participants were remotivated, had improved communication skills and were proactive in seeking in-house training opportunities and promotion.

A follow-up seminar was held for senior managers where the objectives and outcome of the programme were discussed. The initiative thus gained the support of senior managers and the pilot became part of an on-going integrated development programme for female officers. Single-sex training for women in this way became a legitimate organisational activity principally because (i) the initiative produced demonstrable results and (ii) it was effectively sold to managers by the personnel officer.

Management and strategies

Managers have two clear strategies open to them; they are not necessarily EO strategies, but are part of good management practice. The first is setting the targets and goals necessary for the achievement of policy objectives, and guidelines for acceptable behaviour. These must be communicated to staff with the aim of gaining commitment to the achievement of targets and goals. In terms of EO policies this means breaking down policy aims into 'bite size' pieces; it also means giving support to those individuals within departments who are actively pursuing EO policy issues. At a minimal level this means no blocking initiatives, or allowing individuals to become isolated. The second strategy is control; the day may come when individuals will be dismissed for not achieving EO targets and goals, but until that day arrives managers have to tread a fine line between encouragement and censure. 'Encouragement' must be handled sensitively; directives to female members of staff (which often come out of the blue) to go on a training programme for women, worse still one that is concerned with improving personal effectiveness, can, not surprisingly, have a negative effect upon individual women. Thus managers must also be in the business of selling EO policies to their staff. If managers themselves are unclear about what equal opportunities is, what constitutes sexist behaviours, or are ambivalent about their own feelings (initiatives that 'go against the grain'), then it is their responsibility to seek advice and guidance from those who have an exclusive brief to develop EO policies, the equal opportunities officers. (Of course, problems can arise if these individuals are appointed for reasons other than the active development of EO policies.)

Developing managers

Chief officers and senior managers are slowly becoming aware that the severe under-representation of women in top levels of local government management is actually a problem. Several years ago the absence of women in senior positions was an unquestioned fact of organisational life. Shifts in perspectives are occurring, both in the ways women view themselves and in the way men view the world of work. One way of demonstrating the existence of this shift is by simply headcounting the number of high calibre women who applied to participate on executive development programmes aimed exclusively at women principal officers in local government. The programmes were designed and delivered by the Women and Work Programme and focused particularly on those officers who have the potential of moving on to director, deputy director and assistant director posts. It is obvious that women not only felt they met the programmes' criteria, but that their managers who supported their applications also held similar views as to their promotion prospects. Two programmes have run to date and others have been heavily oversubscribed. In terms of the critical mass theory of women's influence upon hierarchies, the response to these Local Government Executive Development Programmes bodes well for positive future changes in the gender balance at the very top of local authority organisational pyramids.

It is usually at this point in a piece of writing (near the end) that it becomes clear how much has been left unsaid, how much there is still to write. From a bird's eye view, the future for taking positive action as a means to achieving equality of opportunity for women in the workplace looks hopeful. Those authorities who have not yet identified equal opportunities as a critical structural and human resource issue will almost certainly come into line with the so-called progressive local authorities. They will have no choice. Alterations in work patterns, demands for specialised and skilled staff, a contracting labour market, will ultimately mean that local authorities will have to compete with other organisations to attract staff. It also means that they will not be able to afford to employ under-utilised staff on which women make up a significantly large proportion – the latent talent on the pay roll. A shortage of labour coupled with the present trend towards increasing organisations' levels of efficiency and effectiveness (see Zehnder, 1984) means that, like it or not, sooner or later employers will have to focus on women.

From a worm's eye view, many women working within local authorities feel less than optimistic. Local authorities, like many other organisations, become overly concerned with verifiability, when confronting contentious or unpopular issues. Thus while it is accepted that women are confined to the bottom of organisational pyramids – simply because they are not in evidence at the top of these pyramids – time has to be spent by individuals within local authorities researching and identifying the obvious, that is gathering statistics to show that this is the case. Having identified the obvious, what is to be done? Knowledge is of no use without the awareness to use it; positive active can help to bridge the knowledge and awareness gap. No matter what level a woman is at within a local authority hierarchy, all women have a responsibility to one another. Only if women are enabled to exercise this responsibility will there be any possibility of real substantive attitude change within organisations. In short, every woman can be another woman's mentor.

3

Behind the scenes: women in television

ANGELA COYLE

Introduction

An evening of armchair research will easily reveal that the vast majority of television programmes on British television[1] are *man* made, even though women make up about one third of the television industry's workforce – far more than programme credits would suggest. It is a highly competitive industry with a large number of technical and specialist occupational functions, which are glamorous, high status, well paid and overwhelmingly occupied by men. Television provides a prime example of gendered job segregation. Women may be a third of the work force but over 60 per cent of all women in television are to be found working in lower graded secretarial/clerical functions, whilst women make up only 8 per cent of senior production staff (Gallagher, 1985b, p. 15). Women in television management are virtually non-existent. Only 3 per cent of senior managers are women – that's approximately one or two women per television company. This chapter looks at the television industry as a gendered and hierarchical form of work organisation in which men occupy most of the key positions of power. It is particularly concerned to look at how this affects women and their experiences of working in the processes of television production which are organised around the experiences and needs of men. It suggests that the organisational form and culture of television production not only excludes women, but reinforces the male experience and helps *reproduce* it. This has meant that the existence of formal equal opportunities since 1975 has had no significant effect in changing the pattern of job segregation in the television industry.

It is argued here that such a male hierarchy as television is maintained despite formal equality because masculinity itself remains an essential qualification and quality required for the occupancy of many key positions within the occupational structure and hierarchy. Leadership and authority remain integrally associated with being a man. This means that many men are uncomfortable even with the idea of women in power over them, whilst not surprisingly, many women select themselves out. The brave few who do pursue technical and managerial grades both jeopardise their feminine status and never quite come up to (masculine) par. This chapter is concerned, therefore, with gender relations in the work place and particularly with the *organisation of work* which effectively institutionalises male power. The existence of gendered job segregation and the concentration of women into 'women's jobs' is the evidence of the way in which being female is defined as somehow 'deficient' and of lower value when set against the male standard. Until women themselves redefine and re-evaluate feminity, equal opportunities for women will sit uneasily, and without great effect, on male-defined organisational structures and hierarchies.

Patterns of segregation

A lot of people and a lot of diverse skills and services contribute to the process of making television, but women, unlike men, display an extraordinary concentration in a very narrow range of jobs. The most comprehensive research that is available on employment patterns in television is a cross national study commissioned by the Commission of the European Communities (Gallagher, 1985a). This research divided the television industry into five major occupational areas in order to analyse occupational segregation.[2] The first of these areas is *production* which is concerned with programme making. This includes the work of producing, directing, operating camera and sound, floor managing, editing, research and journalism. Women make up approximately a quarter of this occupational area, but out of over 150 technical production grades, more than 60 per cent of all women are to be found employed in just three very junior grades: production secretary, ITV production assistance, and continuity girl (sic) (ACTT, 1975, p. 1). The other four major occupational areas are those which support the work of programme making: administration, technical, crafts and services. Not surprisingly, women make up around three-quarters of all *administrative* employees, and here too they are concentrated in lower graded secretarial and clerical jobs. *Technical services*, which covers engineering and technical maintenance, is on the other hand, an almost exclusive male stronghold. For example, the BBC has just 3 per cent of its women employees working in this area. *Craft* occupations comprise such work as design, graphics, wardrobe, make-up, properties and the construction and painting of scenery. In this area women are again in the minority and moreover there is a sharp differentiation between what is considered to be men's work and women's work. Whilst most women are employed in wardrobe and make-up, men predominate as carpenters and painters of scenery.

Finally *Services*, which comprises catering, cleaning, security, receptionists, telephonists, drivers, messengers and general maintenance, does employ large numbers of women. However, here too women are to be found overwhelmingly in typically female work: catering, cleaning and reception, and again the ubiquitous secretarial function.

Job segregation between men and women also operates hierarchically, to the extent that virtually no women are involved in decision making, either about programming or about policy. Of those women working in production, the majority are in junior and typically feminine 'servicing' functions and even amongst those women in administration (the female stronghold), less than 3 per cent are to be found at top management level. Although at a senior level management is a general management function, the route into this level of television administration is still largely via senior technical and production grades (Simms, 1985). Or put another way, senior management is recruited from a pool in which there are virtually no women.

Women employed in television are also less well-paid than men. To an extent this reflects women's junior, low-status position within the organisational hierarchy and the fact that technical and production areas are well organised in trade unions, whilst production schedules (with long working hours) give considerable opportunity for overtime premia. But in her research Gallagher found that even within the same occupational areas men are better paid than women (for example, 'male' craft work is better paid than 'female' craft work) and that even within the same job, such as journalism or research, there is a tendency for women to be employed on a lower part of the scale. In a nutshell, women are employed at a lower pay level for all occupational grades and the more a job is associated with women, the less well-paid it is (ACTT, 1975). This greater value placed on men often begins on entry into the industry and is reinforced thereafter. Gallagher's research found evidence of women being offered jobs with pay set *lower* than the advertised rate. Not only did she find no evidence that this happened to men but, on the contrary, found that there is a tendency for men to be offered salaries *above* the advertised rate (1985a, p. 41).

These patterns of job segregation between men and women have become increasingly entrenched as the industry has developed. During the 1950s and early 1960s, there were relatively more women working in ACTT technical grades in film and television than at any time since (ACTT, 1975). By the late 1960s, the film industry in the UK was in steep decline, and the competition for jobs in the still developing television sector was intense. Women fared badly as a whole range of jobs in television were simply *not open* to women. These included virtually all of the key technical grades: film cameramen and assistants, sound recordists and assistants, lighting assistants, dubbing mixers, film projectionists, film dispatch clerks, studio cameramen, boom operators, floor assistants, gram and tape supervisors, technical managers and video tape editor (Kustow, 1972, p. 65). In 1975, the introduction of the Sex Discrimination Act in the UK made this kind of job closure illegal, and all jobs within television became formally open to both men and women. The gender distribution of jobs has remained constant, however, and reproduced by unchanging patterns of recruitment, training and promotion (Gallagher, p. 17).

Gallagher's research on television identified the two major ways in which women remain particularly disadvantaged in the television career structure. Firstly, women are disadvantaged at the outset by appointment into lower level jobs and secondly, women are promoted less, so over time the gap between men and women actually increases. In comparing a sample of men and women recruits who had entered television at the same time, Gallagher (1985a) found that men fared better than women in every area and at every level. Out of a total of 750 women recruits Gallagher found that 'none actually broke through to the top jobs in the way that men did' (p. 49). Moreover the problem is not simply that women are in areas of employment where career moves are less possible, but even amongst men and women who entered television in administrative jobs, men are *both* more likely to move out into production jobs *and* into more senior administrative positions. The television industry is, then, a prime example of how job segregation between men and women will *not* progressively erode over time. In the absence of positive interventions, it has arguably got worse.

'We are an equal opportunity employer'

All of the major independent television companies and the BBC are now stated equal opportunity employers. Although most do not have a code of practice, nor policy guidelines, and with one or two exceptions, none have made any intervention to change existing practice. The push for some kind of *action* to achieve equal opportunities for women within television has not so much come from employers as from women groups', such as Women in Media,[3] the Women's Broadcasting and Film Industry (WBFI) and the Women's Film, Television and Video Network (WFTVN). In the same way, one of the main unions for the industry, the Association of Cinematograph and Television Technicians (ACTT) has a small but growing women's voice within it.

In recent years, several modest 'landmarks' in the development of equal opportunities within television employment have been achieved. In 1975 the ACTT published a report, *Patterns of Discrimination Against Women in the Film and Television Industries*, which for the first time documented fully the very disadvantaged position of women employed in television. This report was presented to the ACTT Annual Conference that year, and included a series of recommendations for measures to help women working in the industries. These included improved maternity and child care provision, training schemes for women and career counsellling. These recommendations have remained central to ACTT's EO policy ever since.

Later, in 1979, the National Council for Civil Liberties (NCCL) backed with funding from the Equal Opportunities Commission (EOC), persuaded Thames ITV to accommodate a project which sought to achieve equal opportunities for women employees through a series of positive action measures. These included new recruitment and selection procedures, training schemes particularly designed to help women, child care allowances and the appointment of an equality officer (for full details see Thames Television *Equal Opportunities in Employment*, 1983). The project was at that time a considerable intervention and one which went further than anything taking place either within the television industry or outside it.

The setting up of Channel Four in 1980 indisputably changed the scene for television programme making and provided enormous scope for an EO intervention. Unlike either the BBC or the ITV companies, Channel Four does not itself make television programmes. As an organisation it has an essentially administrative function whilst it commissions the making of its programmes from a wide range of small companies, independent film makers and television and film workshops. In adopting a corporate philosophy of innovation and risk taking. Channel Four has given some women *some* opportunity both to make programmes and to represent more positive images of women. Channel Four has always had a very 'up-front' equal opportunities policy statement, due in no small part to the personal commitment of Jeremy Isaacs, Chief Executive of Channel Four, who declared, 'I shall . . . go out of my way to see that women have a stake in the input of the Channel. I shall deliberately arrange that it is so' (WFTVN, 1986). Most importantly Channel Four's policy statement covers both its own practice and that of its programme suppliers:

Channel Four is an equal opportunities employer and is committed to avoiding discrimination in all aspects of employment on grounds of sex, marital status, race or religious beliefs. Channel Four expects its programme suppliers to adopt positive employment policies on these important matters in conformity with the collective agreements appropriate to any engagement. (WFTVN, 1986)

As an employer, however, Channel Four is very small, employing only 200-odd staff. It does employ more women (57 per cent) than men (43 per cent) and it does employ more women at a senior and middle management level than either the BBC or ITV companies. If, however, as a direct employer, Channel Four's scope for effecting changes is limited to its small staff, as a contractor of television programmes its power of influence is potentially enormous. Through the power of contract compliance it can *enforce* equal opportunities practice within all its programme contracts.

Despite this potential, the effects on Channel Four's EO practice has been very limited. There have never been any formal guidelines laid down as to *how* Channel Four should adopt its stated policy and as a result it has been adopted very unevenly. It has meant a preparedness to appoint a handful of women into a few key posts, but power and decision making remains squarely within male-defined parameters; of the 16 directors on the board, 2 are women; of the 3 executive directors, none are women; of the 10 heads of department, 3 are women (WFTVN, 1986, p. 1). Whilst Channel Four does employ a greater proportion of women, this is because as an organisation, it is primarily concerned with administrative service. Of all the women employed at Channel Four, two-thirds are employed in secretarial/clerical functions, and nothing has been done to dismantle this subordinate female role. Moreover, in keeping with the rest of the television industry, it continues to recruit highly qualified and able young women for this work (WFTVN estimates that 50 per cent of all Channel Four secretaries are educated to degree or 'A' level standard), whilst making plain that the company does not expect, nor provide for, any career aspirations amongst this occupational group.

As a commissioner of programmes, Channel Four *has* provided new opportunities for women in television (especially within the Independent Film and Video Department) and this has been done in no small measure through the power and personal commitment of those who hold the Channel's four senior commissioning posts – two of whom are women. However in their survey of Channel Four editors, WFTVN found that whilst some editors did have equal opportunities as one of their principal criteria in dealing with contractors, many did not, and even amongst 'the committed' there were varying ideas about what equal opportunities should mean in practice. What emerges from the Channel Four experience is that very good intentions at the highest level is not enough. The implementation of policy has been left to individual personalities, operating on an ad hoc basis. Now there is evidence that women's involvement in 'the making of programmes for the Channel has *decreased* over time. Where women programme makers have been given work it has tended to be on 'one-off' projects rather than through sustained programming development (WFTVN).

Every one of these initiatives have been very important in trying to overcome women's disadvantaged position within the television industry. But whilst ACTT now has an official commitment to equal opportunities, it still remains a 'women's issue' and very low on the union's agenda; whilst Thames ITV has undertaken a series of measures for women, some years on it is hard to find any real change and men in the company are still very much 'in place'; and whilst Channel Four began with a 'clean slate' and a very strong commitment to equal opportunities, somehow existing practices within the industry have still managed to re-emerge in a new organisational setting.

When the European Commission adopted a Positive Action Programme for 1982–5 it identified the television industry as a critical site for intervention. Cross-national research was commissioned to look at both the employment situation of women in European television companies and at the representation of women in television programmes. This research provided detailed evidence of an employment situation of entrenched job segregation, and considerable barriers to women's career development, and of television programmes which continue to reproduce the most negative stereotypes of feminity (Gallagher, 1985a; Thoveron and Vogel-Polsky, 1985). The research was represented to a conference held in Brussels. Senior management from all European television companies had been invited to attend. In the event few representatives of television management, and indeed few men, attended this conference, and for the most part conference participants were women of fairly junior status, who had been delegated to attend and who were well aware beforehand of the issues and problems they face as women.

Women don't apply

The absence of women in technical and production jobs, effectively excludes women both from making a visible contribution to the industry's product and from its decision making processes. Television management takes no responsibility for this, attributing women's absence to women themselves and their failure to pursue technical qualifications. Fewer girls than boys pursue qualifications in mathematics and science (only one in four), and this then has some reflection in the fact that girls make up only 6 per cent of the BBC's engineering training scheme and in the technical sector as a whole, women occupy only 4 per cent of technical jobs (Gallagher, 1985b, p. 5). It is clearly important, therefore, that more girls are encouraged to maintain the study of mathematics and science at school if they are to enter certain technical occupations. This is especially true when there has been an increasing use in the television industry of formal and technical entry qualifications. However, even if women are 'deficient' in qualifications, this can only provide a partial explanation for their exclusion from technical occupations in television. Often formal qualifications bear little relation to the actual skills required for a particular job and moreover many men in technical occupations in television are not formally qualified. For example, research undertaken by the ACTT found that 50 per cent of sound engineers in television had no formal qualifications and indeed of all men in ACTT, between one-third and two-fifths had no directly relevant qualifications prior to and on entering the industry (ACTT, p. 28). When, as part of their positive action programme, Thames Television undertook research into company entry requirements, it was discovered that 'O' level physics was a requirement for the jobs of cameraman (sic), when none of the men employed in that job were actually so qualified (Herbert, 1985).

In practice, entry into technical and production occupations in television is premised on a shifting mix of formal and informal competences. Entry requirements for many technical/production jobs are often not a question of formal academic study but of having 'fiddled around with radios and tape recorders a lot' (ACTT, p. 6), or of having worked in amateur dramatics. It is these informal, ill-defined entry requirements that particularly disadvantage women. They either draw directly upon a general technical background 'that only exceptional schools and/or parents would encourage their daughter to develop', or a creative background, which is never made explicit in job descriptions. This means that the only women likely to know that they have the ability and background to work in either technical or production grades are those who are already in them (ACTT, p. 28).

Despite these difficulties, there is considerable evidence that women *are* seeking to work in technical and production jobs. Of men and women already in the industry in non-technical grades, far more women than men would like the opportunity to acquire technical skills (ACTT, p. 6), whilst women made up 55 per cent of the 2300 applications (50 places) to the new JOBFIT television apprentices scheme. Outside of the industry, the Women's Film, Television and Video Network (WFTVN) reports of a staggering and ever increasing number of women who are seeking to gain training and experience in television production. A small but increasing number of women are also entering television companies' in-house training. Now there may be one or two women undertaking some form of technical training, whereas previously there would have been none. If it *was* the case that women did not apply for work in technical and production areas, Gallagher suggests that *now* the problem has shifted women do apply and there remains a continued gap between the number of women applicants and the number of female appointments, in all technical and management posts (1985a, p. 42).

The qualifications and qualities that women *are* deemed to possess equip them unfailingly, however, for the secretarial and clerical work which occupies the majority of women working in the industry. It is evident that many women working as secretaries in television have pursued this particular female point of entry, in the belief that this may provide a progressive career route into production jobs. Nothing could be further from the truth. The Simms Report on the BBC (1985) reviewed the career progress of 589 women in secretarial and clerical grades in service over a five-year period (17 per cent of whom were graduates) and found that *only 16* (my emphasis) had moved out of these grades in that period of time. The reason for women's lack of career mobility is not so much their lack of ambition, but the lack of a career structure. Women are actively channelled in this kind of work and find it very difficult to get out of it. At best, secretarial work can lead to the job of production assistant, but thereafter it is *extremely* difficult to move out of this grade and it represents the peak of a female/secretarial career structure. There is no real reason for this since production assistants require considerable production skills and knowledge, and the grade could be an important step in a career path in television production (for both women and men). However, because the job is entirely female, it is invariably dismissed as women's work, as 'just glorified secretaries' and is not integrated into any career ladder (ACTT, p. 29).

As in other media industries (see, for example, Smith, 1976), television lacks formalised or defined career paths. There is no 'typical' way of entering television nor any typical way of developing a career. Research in one television company which looked at the career paths of floor managers (15 in all) revealed that each one had reached that occupation through 15 different sets of qualifications and experience (Callaghan, 1986). This flexibility in career development could be an advantage to women but it does not seem to operate that way. As in floor managing, the route into television directing can be diverse. Directors often have a background in floor managing, camera, editing or research, but whilst the path for research to director is a fairly common one for men, it is very rare for women to progress this way.

Yet directing is a job which particularly requires the qualities of creativity and people management: 'a feeling for television; an ability to express and articulate feeling; objectivity, patience, tact and determination; being good at organising crew and not being too sensitive; management and leadership' (ACTT, p. 29). There is nothing here that should exclude women except that given male domination of technical production areas, this work is essentially the organising, managing and leading male craft technicians. The ACTT report quotes one regional TV manager on why there are so few women in directing: 'I doubt if a woman could control a crew.' This comment is probably more revealing of the social relations of work in television, than it is of women's abilities and qualifications.

Femininity in a man's world

The major occupation of women in television is in the secretarial/clerical support functions. In this acceptable female role, women provide both a key organisational support and a measurement for masculine status: 'An attractive and competent girl secretary is, of course, seen as an asset and status symbol by any man. She is also, often a key support in his professional status' (Simms, p. 18). But women's occupation of this support role to a male hierarchy has very negative effects on women. It degrades their pay and status, but most especially the very nature of the work does little to develop women's sense of their capabilities or worth. Yet television in particular continues to recruit highly qualified and creative women for this work. Secretarial/clerical work is *not* straightforwardly of low skill – as women's relative pay levels would suggest – rather it is a pernicious mix of skill, responsibility and low value. In television, as elsewhere, women's junior administrative function does often combine considerable responsibility for managing people, processes and tasks, with demeaning work such as the continual making, fetching and serving of coffee. Women's level of responsibility is only implicitly and negatively recognised in that a good deal of this work is unsupervised and taken for granted. It *cannot* be explicitly and formally recognised, however, without there being a complete re-evaluation of that work. This would mean a lot more than more pay for women, it would mean that a relationship of power and authority (of men over women) would have to give way to one based on interdependence and equality. Consequently women's work is mostly without any form of positive appraisal and, in the face of a daily taken-for-grantedness, even the most competent of women find their self-esteem plummets, as one senior secretary indicates:

> When I came here [television company] I'd got a degree and good secretarial qualifications, but I got to thinking that I would never be capable of doing anything, or managing anything. I suppose I just didn't have a great deal of confidence in anything I did.

Nor is it only secretarial/clerical employees who are deskilled in this way. The female support function is also integral to the job of Production Assistant, a job which, unsurprisingly, is an exclusively female occupation. It is a job which requires a thorough knowledge of the technical and production aspects of television and therefore production assistants tend to 'know more about television than the men they work for' (Kustow, p. 66). This is not the official view, however, and on the whole these skilled and knowledgeable women are regarded as being there to service the male crew and director. For women to move out of this defined feminine role and acceptable models of femininity they have to make a quantum leap, which is often a greater hurdle than formal entry requirements, or the lack of crèche facilities. It involves leaving behing all popular notions of femininity:

> As a women, I had one mammoth hurdle to jump all at one go. The Director is always Right . . . . For the duration of the rehearsal and recording of a programme you are God, pronouncing, all controlling with a ready answer for all occasions. As women are usually wrong, this meant giving a lie to one's whole existence. (Kustow, p. 62)

It leaves women in a barren zone where they can be neither men nor women. The qualities valued in men are not acceptable in women, whilst the qualities women value are not an acceptable style of working:

> I have worked for several different Heads of Department who might be styled as macho managers. I don't deny that macho management works – through bullying and coercion. Nor would I deny that women can adopt such management techniques. However, I would suggest that many women perceive management as a job that requires certain characteristics that they choose not to adopt – namely a style of management that requires 'balls', as one Head of Department put it. There are other more democratic management styles that involve persuasion and participation that women (and indeed, many people) would find sympathy with . . . . The BBC would benefit from managers who co-operate with each other working for a common good – good programmes, successful networks with high audience figures. (A woman Senior Radio Producer, quoted in Simms, p. 18)

When women move into technical, managerial or production work, as a *small* number of exceptional ability and tenacity do, they create a kind of organisational disequilibrium. How can women be both a low status workforce in low grade jobs, *and* occupy prestigious 'men's' work? It may be that in the future an increasing number of production and technical grades in television will become feminised and deskilled (Braverman, 1974, on clerical work provides the classic case study of this process), but for now women in these jobs are marginalised. They are not real women:

I noticed that the few women I came across or heard of who had 'made the grade' as director were without exception subjected to a battery of personal criticisms. A was an old battle axe who should have retired years ago, B was emotional and impossible to work with, why couldn't C do something about her appearance, D was alright but she hadn't managed to get a husband . . . (Kustow, p. 61)

With this slur cast on their femininity, token women – or pioneers – do *not* necessarily open up the pathway for other women, rather their experience may act as a disincentive: 'As far as I could see, the jungle fight for promotion *wasn't* worth the agony and there wasn't much sweetness and light once you got there, so I stayed thankfully put' (Kustow, p. 61).

Thus working women within television have to find a way of existing within structures and relationships which they have played no real part in defining. The organisational culture of television acts like a gossamer-fine web of low expectancy and lack of opportunity, trapping women in a model of feminine conformity. Women have responded to this situation in a range of different ways. A small number have worked against the odds and have been permitted honorary membership of the male world (provided they keep their noses clean, and never of course with *full* membership privileges). Some adopt a kind of camouflage and whilst seemingly living out an acceptable model of femininity, they subversively chip at institutionalised male power. Many women, however, opt out and with a shrug of the shoulder and the retort of 'television is a man's world', they prefer to lie low, living out the most valued aspects of their lives outside the work place. Who can blame them? Any dissenter reading this will know that along with jeopardising her career opportunities, she has taken on a lifetime's work. The *problem* with quiescence is that it is readily interpreted as consensus, when it is not, and as a strategy it does not provide obvious guidelines for action. As Rowbotham (1972) has written, 'women have been lying low for so long most of us cannot imagine how to get up' (p. 5).

Acting for a change

The existence of legislation which gives women formal rights with men and the principle of equality of opportunity now 'exposes' this ongoing inequality in the work place. What it does not provide however is a strategy for effective interventions which will change this situation; there is no blueprint for ensuring equality of opportunity *and* similarity of outcome; there is no model for organisational change of this kind.

When surveying the totality of women's organisational disadvantage it is hard to know how and where to begin. The enormity of the task and the range of issues (both inside and outside of the work place) do not themselves suggest forms of intervention which may be undertaken by women, usually working in isolation. It is worth noting therefore that a Positive Action Project now being undertaken by the Women and Work Programme, in one of the major independent television companies, began with one woman setting up a woman's group.

A feature of the Women's Movement of the late 1960s and early 1970s in both Britain and the United States was the small autonomous women's group. In an unstructured way women came together to explore their experiences as women. Through these 'consciousness-raising groups' women began both to find a language in which to express *women's* experiences and consciousness, and to imagine other ways of being. Since then, avowedly 'feminist' activity has moved in a diverse range of directions, including more externally focused activities. When a number of women working for a particular ITV company came together as a women's group, they probably would not have responded to the idea of the group as either a 'feminist' or a consciousness-raising activity. Meeting outside working hours but in the workplace, the formal agenda for this group was to discuss work-related issues. Yet women came to the group with thoughts previously unformulated and unspoken and somehow, a women's consciousness-raising group entered the workplace. Three very different women illustrate their discovery of a specific need:

I saw the notice on the board and it had immediate appeal. I needed this group in order for me to be able to air views that I'd got and talk with women of a like mind.

Really I didn't have anything specific in mind, just like a lot of other people, this niggling thing at the back of my mind, I don't like being a secretary.

When you start off you really do realise that a lot of people feel the same way. It put the whole thing into perspective. That it is a big issue, it's not just something I was concerned with, it was something that every women should be concerned with. Finding that I wasn't the only person who thought like that, there were other people who raised exactly the same thoughts and fears and aspirations as my own.

Participating in such a group as this, in the context of the workplace, has not always been easy and both the group as a whole and individuals within it have been the focus of much curiosity and sometimes derision (from women as well as men). But the gains have been greater, the group has provided friendship and support and a growing appreciation that their individually-experienced disadvantage is actually a collective one. This group's discussions have ranged over the universal concerns of women in work from the lack of career structure and opportunities for women, lack of opportunities for training, and the low value placed on women's work, childcare, housework, to men – at work and at home. It has provided women with the space to develop an understanding of their experiences and in which they have *shifted the problem* away from their own failures as individual women to identify the far wider processes by which women's opportunities are structured and constrained: 'I see the problems of schooling, discrimination in schooling and the lack of encouragement for the girls. I'd like to do some work with children at school, at thirteen, when they are choosing their options' (secretary and group member).

As this group has continued it has shared skills and knowledge as well as providing mutual support. Women have helped each other with work, job applications and career moves. It has also developed an external focus and has 'established' the group in the eyes of the company management in a range of ways. Some women have sought meetings with their own managers to raise with them issues relating to women's situations within television, the group as a whole set up a series of meetings with directors of the company. These activities have not been particularly easy either, since it involves a degree of self-exposure and visibility that many men would not risk. But for some women at least 'standing up to be counted' has become a personal project:

I think many women are frightened to voice their views. I think

that's been quite apparent from the meetings we've had with
Senior Management. It's mainly the very strong ones of us that
have been asked questions, although there's been a lot of people
who voiced off at me afterwards, in the corridor, but were too
frightened to open their mouths at the meeting . . . . It's shyness,
it's a fear of standing up and saying, of being identified. I
understand. When I stood up for the first time I was shaking but
you have to do it, you feel you have to do it. You cannot have a
director talk to you and not respond. (group member).

The women's group in this television company does not probably
appreciate how important it has been as an agency for change. They
have stepped outside and away from stereotypes of femininity and
feminine quiescence; they have been seen and heard, they have
raised a voice of dissent. It was their presence, and this voice, that
helped make the case for running a short three-day training course
for women only with the company. This *personal development*
training course provided 15 women with the opportunity to explore
over 3 days issues relating to employment, to their lives outside
work, and to develop skills and approaches which would enable
them to be more effective at work. It provided another occasion for
women to come together and, as a highly participative course, it
again enabled women to find a voice. Some of the course
participants were from the women's group, but many were not, so
the course was also an occasion for widening this emerging
collectivity amonst women. The demand for this course was so high
that a subsequent course was run.

At this point, with this kind of momentum *generated by women*, it
was possible for the Women and Work Programme to propose to
this Company that they undertake a *Women's Development Project*.
With the support of the personnel department and a very committed
company director, this proposal was accepted and a wide range of
activities are now underway. The scope of the activity has
broadened to ensure the inclusion of women at all grades (including
manual staff) and to involve men. This now very much larger
activitity still adheres to its original philosophy: that small changes
can have big effects. Work in progress now includes a series of
training activities for women, as well as opportunities for technical
and managerial observation placements and training secondments.
There are two staff working parties: one made up of women staff,

representative of all grades and occupations; the other is made up of management, men and women. Both groups have set their own agenda and are working both in their own departments and across the company to develop new forms of working practice which will help overcome women's disadvantage.

It is too soon to assess how effective this particular positive action project has been in making change; early successes have to be set against some of the formidable barriers that this chapter has outlined.

Making up the rules and moving the goal posts

It is very important that women are now identifying the ways in which they are disadvantaged within formal organisational procedures and structures. Because it is men who occupy key organisational positions their actions and processes usually reflect male norms and priorities. The most obvious ways in which women are disadvantaged is in the way that work organisation still takes little or no account of parental responsibilities. Work place childcare facilities and part-time working arrangements (which *can* integrate into a career structure) are virtually non-existent. Perceived as 'women's needs' such measures are regarded as costing money, not fitting into television production schedules and anyway women have to fit in with the world, not have special concessions made for them. Whilst male organisational priorities are perhaps manifested in different structural forms as the Simms Report quotes: 'a woman television reporter expressed surprise that the BBC had no crèche, "when it has a bar in every building, providing a large debilitating drinking pool, subsidised for the ill health of its employees" . . .' (p. 18).

The refusal to recognise family responsibility in the workplace is a very real issue for women, given that women are in the main responsible for such care. Nevertheless it is my impression that most women feel they can manage that duality in their lives. What is much harder is the systematic under-evaluation of women's work and abilities and their inferior status and lack of power vis à vis men. It is this which remains virtually untouched by equal opportunities. Whilst most television companies have introduced more formalised recruitment procedures to help facilitate equal opportunities, it is still the case that the majority of senior appointments in television are made without open competition (Gallagher, 1985a; Simms, 1985). 'Getting on' is actually achieved through a system of informal patronage, and hence the patronage of men. Women are not absolutely excluded from this but it acts as a form of (male) control, as a woman assistant editor has observed: 'If I'd made a fuss [over discriminatory practice) I'd have got as name as a loud-mouthed trouble maker and no one would have offered me a job' (ACTT, p. 3). Moreover, the *myth* of formalised selection places women in a double bind. Since selection is stated to be open and competitive women are wary of any form of positive 'discrimination' for women, as this may be construed as women's inability to compete. Yet, as appointments to mangement grades are so often made on the 'old boy network' (Simms, p. 18), the reality is that women are competing in a system where positive discrimination for men is the norm.

This kind of double standard is possible in organisation hierarchies through which male power is institutionalised. Through a range of structures men still have the power to define how the organisation will operate in ways which· reflect their interests. Policies designed to advantage women will not necessarily be acted upon. One of the effects of the introduction of equal opportunities has been to illustrate the split in organisations, between what is *formally* supposed to take place and what actually happens. As with the split in formal and informal selection procedures, so with decision-making processes. Research commissioned by the EEC on the television industry found that where some women had moved into managerial decision-making grades, so the site of the decision-making process has moved elsewhere (Vogel and Zaid, 1985, p. 36). That men are not working to facilitate equal opportunities for women should be no surprise. Work hierarchies are the place where gender identities are lived out daily. Masculinity is partly defined by men's power in relation to women; equal opportunities for women can seem like the loss of power *and* manhood itself. Thus through a range of different mechanisms women are daily kept 'in place'. Most men simply cannot comprehend that this happens, let alone how it occurs. Working with men in television I have been struck by how little they know of women and how little they realise the effects of their own practice. They participate knowingly and unknowingly in a system of privilege. At an individual level, most men would not feel that they possess power or enjoy privilege. Men's strength lies in the way in which an ideology of gender, of expectations of masculinity and femininity, is lived out in the *collective practice* of an organisation.

Women too live out these gendered expectations and the construction of femininity also makes 'equality' for us double-edged; it could be construed as the rejection of being a woman. What is clear, however, is that gender ideology which confines women to subordinate roles corresponds less and less to the reality of experience. In the family an increasing number of women are either the main wage earner, or a wage earner of equal contribution and this gives the lie to the assertion that women are confined to the bottom of the organisational hierarchy because of their prior commitment to the family responsibilities (see Fogarty *et al.*, 1971, for the 'classic' exposition of why there are no women in 'top jobs' in television). This centrality of women's paid work and, indeed, their career aspirations has little form of expression in the television industry. Women still enter, in droves, typically female jobs in secretarial and clerical functions, ones which seemingly *confirm* the stereotype of femininity. What has not been articulated is the way in which women enter this kind of work in the belief that it is the route to a career. As one television secretary of 15 years stated: 'I thought if I was a secretary, then I'd make the jump off!' Women are still drawn to 'women's jobs' in television in the absence of realistic career counselling (see Deem, 1978), and seem to reconcile 'popular notions of femininity' (see Sheratt, 1983, for a full discussion of girls career aspirations and 'glamour') with career aspirations:

> I mean you apply for a secretarial job not because you specifically want to do that work, but because it's television, because it sounds exciting. I think it would be very difficult to expect an 18 year old to say 'Yes, I want to work for television because I want to work for the Lighting Director' because she won't know what it is. (Television secretary)

The continuing problem for women is that they still only discover the lack of career structure in 'women's jobs' through experiencing them: 'You realise you can do something else and you know there's no way out. Once you're a secretary that's it.' By the time women realise the limiting nature of the 'choices' they've made, it is very difficult to overcome them in a structure which does not easily permit either a second chance or a change in consciousness.

Whilst formal equality for women has been critical, discourse on equal opportunities and positive action strategies has taken place on a level which has been focused at achieving 'equality' between men and women through the establishment of formal rights and equal representation in the labour market. Whilst there has been within this discourse a recognition of both the formal and the informal barriers which exclude women from certain occupational areas and occupational power, it remains rooted in an essentially meritocratic, rationalistic and liberal ideology. It is under-pinned by the *supposed* existence of a socially just, meritocratic society and that the continued manifestation of inequality between men and women is an unacceptable leftover from a previous epoch. In this liberal ideal there is no room for a society fundamentally divided, and in potential conflict, through divisions of *class* and *gender* and *race*. In this assumption of all things being equal it is, in some ways, *harder* to speak out against discrimination – it doesn't exist.

Despite the containment of equal opportunities and strategies for positive action, it has opened up a space for women to look at the world differently; to reassess it and their place within it. Women working in television are coming together to support each other in their quest for training skills and the re-evaluation of their work. Since television in addition to being an employer of women is the crucial medium in our society for the representation of male and female gender ideology, they have a particularly vital task.

Notes

1. This has been taken to include the providers of the four major TV Channels in Britain; the BBC, the Independent Television Companies (who form the Independent Television Companies Association (ITCA)) and Channel Four. It does not include the small independents who may be sub-contracted by these Channels.
2. The five occupational areas drawn up by Gallagher are used here as they are useful in sorting the confusion of jobs in television. However, they are only a guide since not all jobs fit easily into these categories and there are some jobs which could fit into more than one category.

3. Women in Media are not only active within their own sector. They were also one of the most prominent women's groups involved in the campaign for the introduction of equal rights legislation in the UK.

4

Pin money professionals?
Women in teaching

ELISABETH AL-KHALIFA

Women have constituted the majority of the teaching force in British schools for most of this century, forming between 60 per cent and 70 per cent of teachers. Teaching is conventionally associated with women, but educational leadership is viewed as essentially men's work.

Such a division of teacher work by sex is not recent, and reflects the history of girls' and boys' education, and the differentiated roles for men and women in this. In 1983, Department of Education and Science statistics showed that only 16 per cent of headteachers in secondary schools in England and Wales were women, whereas 63 per cent of Scale One teachers and 50 per cent of Scale Two teachers were women. In primary schools, although women made up 78 per cent of teachers, only 44 per cent of headships were held by women, but 92 per cent of Scale One teachers and 83 per cent of Scale Two teachers were women.

Looking back over the years, the situation of women teachers has deteriorated despite the common belief that 'things are getting better'. In 1965, 23.7 per cent of secondary heads were women, and 50.8 per cent in primary schools.

The situation of women teachers, far from improving since the Sex Discrimination Act 1975, has declined.

At the same time, growing interest in equal opportunities has led to policy declarations by some employing authorities, supported in a few cases by the appointment of an advisor or advisory teacher for gender, but usually with inadequate resources for the scope of the task. Within this, the focus has naturally been on the curriculum but teacher employment and discrimination has also been addressed, through reviewing selection and promotion procedures. However, the experience of sexism and gender stereotyping impinges on all aspects of teacher work, and it is this which positive action has to address. The aim of this chapter is therefore to attempt to map out what this might mean in practice for women teachers, especially in their daily work in schools, as well as in the operation of the education service as a whole.

Women's work, men's work

Explanations offered for women teachers' under-representation in senior posts range from research-based material to the speculative mythology which surrounds discussion of gender roles. Byrne (1978) rehearses much of this discussion in her treatment of the situation of women teachers. She draw attention to the way in which women teachers are represented as preoccupied with marital security, childcare and husbands' careers. Child rearing, the inevitable destination of the woman teacher, necessarily leads to a career break, which in turn results in women teachers holding lower paid, less responsible posts, clustering in the primary sector. Women teachers are consequently thought to have a low commitment to teaching as a career and to career advancement. Such an account of women teachers' careers thus views parenting (by women) as incompatible with professional work.

Accounts of women teacher's careers have tended to be couched in terms of a preoccupation with motherhood accompanied by a low level of professional commitment. This valuation had been institutionalised by the marriage bar on women operating in teaching until after the Second World War, and was a view endorsed by the National Association of Schoolmasters in their resistance to equal pay for women teachers. Men, by contrast, have been thought to represent the professional norm, strongly motivated in their careers, understood in terms of a clear promotion orientation, underpinned by an attributed role of 'breadwinner'. Such views are not restricted to research studies and official reports, but are pervasive, shared by teachers, parents, and employers alike.[1]

Byrne, however, offers other kinds of explanations for women's non-promotion. She speculates that secondary school reorganisation with continuing upheavals, greater organisational complexity accompanied by rapidly increasing external demands on teachers and the curriculum, have deterred women as a group from applying for promotion. She attributes this to a reluctance in women to engage in decision-making and conflict. This explanation sits uneasily with the evident success of women heads at large girls' comprehensives and their presence in leadership roles in single sex schools. However, commentators offer suggestions of barriers which may impede women's promotion including the possibility that male teachers are better qualified, that they are better placed for promotion because of the subjects taught, which are linked to large departments and greater responsibility, and that they have more extensive experience than women.

Many of these kinds of explanations outlined share common features. Firstly, they treat women teachers as a homogeneous group – a type with uniform characteristics. Thus women are married (or about to marry) and caring for children (or about to do so). This typification then becomes the fundamental explanatory factor for their career behaviour from which other explanations are then derived, such as low career orientation.

Secondly, women teachers are identified as a group in terms of failure – failure, that is, to fit a model of professional behaviour which is ascribed to men and valued. This model is one of a teacher who has a strong promotion orientation, and a commitment to work beyond the classroom role. In this view, women shrink from such behaviours, engrossed in child care concerns, lacking drive and ambition. Thirdly, the part of men in this analysis is minimal. Their marital status is not a matter for note, their childcare role is ignored, and their ascribed values are not researched.

The characterisation of women teachers as married with children is demolished by a survey conducted by the National Union of Teachers (NUT) into women teachers' careers with a sample of 2829 women (NUT/EOC). Their findings stress the diversity of this group and point out that the category of women married with children was equalled by the number of women who were single parents and those who had dependent relatives to care for. The survey also found no evidence for the claim that women teachers had a low promotion orientation or that marriage and family altered this. A smaller scale survey of women and men by the NUT (1984) in Coventry concluded that a significant proportion of the difference between the scale positions of men and women 'is related to the sex of the teacher, suggesting that men are favoured candidates in the promotional hierarchy' (NUT, p. 29).

Another large-scale survey of teachers' career patterns was conducted by the Inner London Education Authority (ILEA) with a sample of 2510 women and men from secondary schools. This study provides further elaboration of our knowledge about working patterns among teachers. It found that the argument that long career breaks accounted for lower scale positions of married women could not be sustained since more than half of those taking a break were out of teaching for five years or less. Women in the sample did indeed make fewer applications for promotion than men as a group, but it was observed that only a third of the difference between men and women could be accounted for by women intending to start a family. Although women and men are both influenced as a group by the same factors in their attitudes to promotion, women, it seemed, were more discriminating:

> Men appear to regard promotion as more of a desirable, and maybe, inevitable, event in its own right. Women, while by no means uninterested in promotion, are more likely to weigh the quality of the job they are doing at present against the benefits that any promotion might bring. (ILEA, 1984, p. 8)

The study found evidence that women with a partner and children made fewer applications than single women and the partner's career was viewed as more important. However, it also noted that this point had to be set against the finding of a general reluctance among both men and women to move house, with similar reasons given irrespective of sex. Moreover a sizeable percentage of men and women teachers (15 per cent) was interested in job-sharing, most commonly to gain time and reduce stress.

The ILEA study and the various NUT and EOC studies reveal a broadening of the discussion of women teachers' careers, not surprisingly, since they originated from a concern for equality. They indicate a more complex picture of men's, as well as women's, career paths and preferences. Above all, these studies raise the question of sex discrimination as one significant factor on explaining differences between the position of women and men in salary scale, in marked contrast, for example, with the Department of Employment, which saw this concentration of women on lower scales as self-explanatory.

You can't sing bass'[2]

Studies have shown a widespread belief among teachers that sex discrimination exists in teaching and teacher employment. In the ILEA Survey, 55 per cent of women teachers thought that women were discriminated against (compared with 40 per cent of men in the sample who thought this), and 32 per cent of the women thought that discrimination would occur in the appointment of senior posts (compared with 3 per cent of men). Rosemary Grant's study of men and women teachers in Sheffield finds evidence of a similar feeling among women teachers, although she found no statistically significant difference between women and men in the number of complaints of sex discrimination at interview (Grant, 1984, 1986).

The view is confirmed by the evidence provided in industrial tribunal cases brought by teachers invoking the 1975 Sex Discrimination Act. Despite the severe difficulties individuals encounter in pursuing tribunal cases, teachers have successfully proved sex discrimination (Kant, 1985). These cases have involved instances of discriminatory questions at interview relating to family (Gates *v.* Wirral) and faulty and discriminatory procedures at the short-listing stage (Hay *v.* Lothian). In the well publicised case of Chadwick *v.* Lancashire County Council, discrimination was proved, but the tribunal also ruled that Vera Chadwick, a deputy head applying for headships, had been victimised when she complained of sex discrimination.

The extent to which selectors persist in asking illegal and discriminatory questions of women candidates reveals the sex stereotyping which persists in views of women teachers, and of men. In the survey of promotion prospects, by the West Kent Association of the NUT, almost 1 in 5 women was asked questions about marriage plans or childcare arrangements (compared with 1 in 17 men). The questions followed a pattern familiar from previous research, such as: 'Does your husband agree to your working?', 'Are you likely to become pregnant in the near future?', but also included provocatively sexist assumptions as in 'You do realise that if you take this job you won't be able to have time off for a hair-do or to go shopping' (*Times Educational Supplement*, February 19, 1986).

The impertinence and irrelevance of such questions is a clear reminder of how the image of women teachers remains first and foremost one of wives and mothers, irrespective of marital status, life stage, proven experience and demonstrated professionalism. In the face of legislation against sex discrimination, selection processes are still wide open to abuse and prejudice.

Proving the extent of this problem is difficult in the face of extensive prejudice, and as Kant (1985) shows, this extends to the tribunals themselves. Her study of tribunal case decisions related to teachers makes clear the subjectivity of such tribunal proceedings. The members of these work with biased assumptions about men and women's roles and with the kind of sex stereotypes which are precisely those under judgement.

We also know from the Project on the Selection of Secondary Headteachers (POST) that recruitment and selection in education is lamentably underdeveloped (Morgan *et al.*, 1983). This research, conducted into LEA practices, showed that selection is usually carried out in an amateurish and inconsistent manner. As a result, selection procedures are likely to be inequitable, and it is not surprising, therefore, that women teachers feel that sex discrimination and bias are commonplace.

For many women teachers, sex discrimination in selection and promotion is a fact – and acknowledged feature of employment, and in practice, there seems to have been little movement from the situation described by a woman teacher in the NUT survey in 1980: 'I never cease to be amazed that women are penalised for having children but men are promoted because they have a family to support.' The difficulties that many women do encounter in maintaining dual roles, combining the work of family care responsibilities with a full commitment to paid teaching work, a situation which women themselves recognise as demanding and often stressful, is not acknowledged in the assessment of a teacher's worth. On the contrary, this combination of professional and family care roles is viewed only negatively.

When women take a career break, they are usually penalised by a reduction in status and pay and promotion opportunities. It is common for a woman returner to find re-entry to teaching possible only on the lowest salary scale, irrespective of previous levels of seniority and responsibility, or alternatively, if she takes part-time work, this is conventionally offered only at the bottom scale. Worse still, in many cases, women returners may only be offered temporary contracts or a supply teaching position, ensuring for the employer a readily disposable pool of labour, but an insecure situation for the woman and one which devalues her skills and experience. This indirect discrimination is not recognised as such despite the large numbers of teachers involved and the waste of skilled resources.

'Doing right and feeling bad'[3]

(Much of the material used in this section is drawn from work undertaken by a number of participants in the School Management Development and Women Teachers Project, (SMDWT). This work consisted of in-service activities, personal interviews and survey work led by headteachers and teachers in their schools, primary and secondary, with men and women colleagues.

Ann Oakley has drawn our attention to the structural ambivalence that surrounds women's positions and character in industrial society. She argues that 'feminine' characteristics are simultaneously negatively and positively evaluated, through stereotypes, through the actual behaviour of women and their own self-perceptions (Oakley, 1981). This insight contributes to our understanding of the position of women teachers and their experience of work. without this, it is difficult to reconcile women's achievement as teachers with their lack of recognition, status, financial reward and power within the education system.

Working within this system, in which sex hierarchies are explicitly and implicitly embodied in curriculum and organisation, women teachers appear to work with quite clear ideas of competence and worth. In addition to offering precise definitions of valued teacher qualities relating to classroom teaching and the class teacher's role in the school, women teachers specifically identify activities which they argue should not be considered criteria of competence, notably extra-curricular activities (and within these, training football teams!)

An interesting aspect of these definitions is their clarity and specificity, which reflects a considerable degree of self-evaluation. On the other hand, interviews and discussions with male teachers generally do not spontaneously yield these kinds of mental maps of competence, but rather, an almost formulaic perception of personal readiness for promotion irrespective of career stage.

Emerging from this process of self-evaluation among women teachers are strong indications of a sense of competence and pride and their work. Nowhere in schools is women teachers' conviction of the value of their contribution to children's education more evident than in the very part of the school system which carries the lowest status, the poorest pay and promotion prospects – the nursery and infant sector. Infant teachers would appear to subscribe to a common core of values which suggests a positive view of their role. King (1978), in his study of the infant school, indicates the nature of these values when he concludes that the infant teacher is someone who believes in developmentalism, individualism, play as learning and 'childhood innocence'.

Women teachers' evident pride in their work is nonetheless not unqualified. Two other themes emerge when they reflect on their work which reveals the conditional nature of their self-assessment. Firstly, again and again, in interviews, surveys, group discussions, and in training events, women teachers register their concern about the range of roles they feel committed to in addition to their teaching role. Women teachers express anxieties about maintaining other priorities and commitments to their satisfaction alongside their responsibilities in paid work. These other responsibilities, real and anticipated, include child care, care of other dependents, sustaining relationships with partners or other close relatives, and domestic work. These represent demands or pressures which, to a greater or lesser degree, can conflict with the requirements that they feel arise from their job.

These different roles are not perceived as discrete but impinge on the continuing assessment a woman may make of her work and of its direction. Different spheres of action connect – the personal and the professional merge and the meanings of both are not experienced necessarily as distinct, but within a common context. Competence, therefore, is not defined in relation to the one area of activity only, that is, teaching, but is in the context of several dimensions of experience, in a set of interdependent roles, all of which contribute to self-definitions of competence.

Women teachers reported here have voiced their search to achieve a balance which they seek to realise in their lives between a number of roles, but frequently find this a source of stress and even of guilt. However, their actual conditions of employment, the ethos of their schools, the persistence of sex-role stereotyping, and the reality of the division of work in the home can all contribute to constructing an environment which is insensitive or even antagonistic to the aspirations of women teachers.

The attempt to integrate a variety of roles in ways compatible with an internalised image of an ideal 'feminine' life can be fraught with conflict. The outcome may be a sense of personal shortcomings. Women teachers can be severe in the judgements they make of their own achievement, thereby also limiting their sense of efficacy and their future choices. By contrast, men teachers involved in discussion and interview indicate a kind of detachment from domestic and other roles, however they may have understood these. Indeed, questions about the relationship between home and work appear to be puzzling for some men teachers, even when their attention is drawn to this, certainly in the terms women seem to understand these relations.[4]

A second theme appearing in women's thinking about their work and competence is an ambivalence and unease which turns on self-doubt and a sense of personal limitations, which the interview anecdote quoted earlier encapsulates. Women's self-perceptions are inextricably bound up with social norms about women's roles and women's work, and the groups of infant teachers cited above pinpoint some of this uncertainty. They draw attention to how the very features of their work which are a source of satisfaction and pride for them are precisely those which diminish their worth in the eyes of others:

> Is it because infant teachers are caring, encouraging learning to be a pleasurable activity involving parents, staff and children that they feel undervalued? . . . Infant teachers are expected to teach a full range of subjects, to be responsible for social training (including toilet training, tying shoelaces). This portrays a 'motherly' image therefore we are regarded as CHILD

MINDERS and not professionals. (Summary of their staff discussion of infant teaching by a group of Infant Teachers)

The convergence of maternalism and servicing in teachers' work, while especially striking in the nursery and infant phase, is a present feature throughout the education system, and institutionalised in schools' pastoral organisation. However, the ways in which the curriculum is organised and teaching roles and responsibilities divided along sex-stereotyped lines, result in a continuing association of women with these functions which have such low social status.

Apart from teaching, other functions carried out by women in education in support services merely serve to emphasise this: cooking, cleaning, typing, 'looking after' the headteacher, and generally clearing up on the school site. The areas of education where the servicing elements are most marked (nursery, infant) are those that men avoid, unless, as in the case of primary schools, there is the possibility of 'specialising' in teaching a restricted age range, such as the 10–11 year old pupils, and of easy access to leadership posts, of deputy and headteacher. Similarly, in secondary schools, women may be entrusted with the discipline and welfare of younger pupils and girls, but men are recruited for older pupils. 'Growing up', it would seem, brings status; competence and pupil age become confused.

The allocation of tasks and the organisation of schools on a gender role basis is linked to a hierarchy of status and financial reward which signals clearly to all a hierarchy of competence founded on sex differentiation. Pupils themselves appreciate this point – 'When you grow up, you'll be able to teach juniors, won't you, miss?', and it is not surprising that we find women teachers internalising these values to some extent. The infant teachers referred to above indicated their felt need for male colleagues, in the belief than men teachers must inevitably, as men, improve the standard and quality of the staff's work.

Further examination of the reasoning behind this revealed the kind of qualities attributed to men teachers – less parochial, a better sense of humour, a broader outlook, higher standards. Wavering between a recognition of their own self-worth, and deference to men credited with virtues which by implication the teachers were denying themselves, these discussions demonstrate the trap women constantly operate in, of ambivalence about the limits of their competence, which a sex role ideology fuels.

Low or limiting self-esteem may have its roots in early socialisation. Dependence, deference and co-operation on unequal terms are as much a part of the school staffroom as they are of any other social situation or interaction among women and men. On the other hand, this does not represent mere acquiescence on the part of women. What goes unremarked by men especially, in the life of schools is the manner in which men as a group actively assert their claim to authority, greater competence and public esteem, in ways which continuously restate and reaffirm unequal roles, in the face of conflicting aspirations and demands by women. Even if a woman teacher begins her career with a sense of efficacy and purpose, or gradually perceives the reality of her situation in schools, the behaviour and attitudes of many men, and especially those men who establish the ethos of the school and staffroom, ensures a lack of support within the school and in other work-related situations which limits her performance.

For many men, the pre-eminence of men is not in doubt, and women are expected to share and acknowledge this vision.

Two schools were subject to a proposed amalgamation, one infant, one junior. There was a female deputy in the Infants, and a male deputy in the Juniors. The male deputy suggested to the other that if the amalgamation took place, then he should become the new Deputy, while she should become head of the Infant department (Headteacher account).

The right to promotion is the clearest manifestation of this, and is constantly asserted in a variety of means:

Three Scale 3 posts existed in a school – two men and one woman. An inspector visited the school. The headteacher brought the male inspector into the staffroom and introduced the two male Scale 3 teachers but not the female. The inspector told the head that the men should be thinking of promotion (Headteacher account).

The experience of teaching may, at one level, be immensely rewarding for women teachers, but the interaction of male and female staff, and contact with other males – parents, advisors, governors, and pupils – can serve to exclude women, to deny their achievement, and to denigrate them. The effects of this can percolate through to all female staffs, and in any case are coincidental with similar experiences in non-work settings. The starting point for this process in schools is the esteem in which 'masculine' values and characteristics and masculinity itself are held. As a consequence, while women and men are locked into the appearance of co-working, women are, in fact, often regardless of formal status, and their numbers, constituted by men as an 'outgroup' and pushed to the margins of the school as an organisation.

Man – 'the active virtue'[5]

Relationships among teachers, professional norms of behaviour and of competence, are pervaded with notions of innate male superiority and male as norm. The 'masculine aura of competence' that Tolson (1977) refers to in his study of masculinity has an ideal setting in schools – in the classroom, in the corridors, in the school assembly, and in the staffroom, with a group of conscript spectators, and in an environment of sociability.

Every opportunity is provided by the school as a workplace for the male teacher to work through a kind of 'performance' which invokes his masculine affiliation and the power accruing to the male sex. The movement, dress and deportment of men teachers in the playground and the staffroom all contribute to this. The dark-suited men clustering portentously in corridors are actively engaged in projecting a male presence, and the intended audience is women as well as pupils.

Observation of teacher interaction in school suggests that this kind of performance is indeed acted out by male teachers. In so doing, they sustain their dominant role, drawing on their power in their collective identity as men, and as individuals through their occupation of senior positions in the school hierarchy. Berger (1972) observes that such male presence has no equivalent for women, and he suggests that *men act* and *women appear*. From the vantage point of a man, this may necessarily seem the case: the male interpretation of men and women's behaviour depicts women as passively endorsing the male drama. It is no coincidence that in many mixed secondary staffrooms, men, like boys, occupy more physical space, engage in activities which dominate the staffroom area, such as darts or card games, making occasion sorties into quieter zones with noisy horseplay. All this reinforces an impression of male centrality, just as in the classroom, if teachers pay attention to girls, boys engage in distracting activities. Such activity serves to emphasise a sense of male agency with women outside the magic circle as mere spectators.

The attribution of agency to men and passivity to women underestimates the extent to which men work hard to create this impression, in front of each other, no less in schools than elsewhere. Moreover, women act, but the force and validity of their actions is denied by their male colleagues, or appropriated.

In schools, this aspect of male/female interaction is most visible in the area of pupil control. The curricular implications of teachers' preoccupations with order and pupil discipline have been well researched. Pupils' discipline is an organisational priority. Male pupils especially are seen as a potential threat to order and the ability to deal with this threat is thought by school managers (and employers) to rest in the hands of male staff. Despite classroom evidence to the contrary, men are credited with this ability as a group, because of a belief in the inherent authority of a male presence. In schools, male presence is then bound up with attributions of physical strength which in turn confers on all men the right to command and to control. On this basis, men are assumed by interviewers and heads of schools to be ideally suited for senior pastoral posts as well as deputy headships and headships in primary schools. In contrast, women, are believed to lack such qualities: 'I was told by the head of school that women were never really considered as Head of Upper School as they hadn't got the physical strength to cope with boys of this age' (teacher, secondary school). Another teacher reports how, at an interview for a senior management post in a sixth-form college, she was asked how she would cope with male pupils since she was 'too short'.

The reference to control of boys as a significant criterion for promotion is in itself an interesting commentary on current ideas of professional competence, disregarding as it does the girls, and the contribution of curriculum content, teacher attitudes and methodology to pupil behaviour and ethos. The association of pupil control and discipline with implied acts of violence by male teachers is a disturbing cultural norm which raises questions about the kind of ethos we would wish our schools to demonstrate. Nevertheless, pupil control remains in many schools the touchstone for success, the mark of professional competence and it is overtly linked with masculinity.

Male 'performance' comes into its own in building reputations and announcing male credentials to control. Women teachers constantly report and deplore the interference by male colleagues in their classrooms, when male colleagues enter uninvited to 'discipline' particular pupils in their presence, because the male teacher has judged that the female is in need of some kind of assistance. The message such intrusions are intended to convey to pupils and teacher alike is a belief on the part of the male teachers in their capacity for more effective action. It is also a statement that the male teacher perceives his professional relationship with the woman as one of inequality, indicating the woman's subordination, since such interference would normally be viewed as unprofessional amongst peers.

When men teachers draw attention to their controlling role through interventions in women teachers' areas of responsibility, or gratuitously taking on such a role in public parts of the school, they are undoubtedly engaged in demarcating a male zone. Such interventions go beyond asserting the prior rights or greater competence of men in discipline. They are a claim for credibility and prestige in the eyes of authority; they project a belief in male rights to that authority, and in many cases, they are a kind of theft of women teacher's own authority and claims to recognition:

We form-tutors were expected to accompany our classes to Year Assembly twice a week and to keep them quiet until the Head or a senior teacher arrived to take the assembly. Usually I was first to arrive in the hall with my class so obviously I would 'maintain order' as the other classes filtered in. Another colleague, male, would inevitably arrive last and take up position beside me at the front of the hall glowering at the children as if, by his mere – late – presence, order had been achieved. He always managed to get to the hall just before the Headteacher so that it appeared he had been there all along and was absolutely in control (Scale 2 female teacher, secondary).

Such emphatic visibility underpins a general conviction of the rights of men to hold senior positions and to command women. It may also erode some women's sense of competence, and does antagonise others who see such display as unprofessional and patronising.

Male presence is not only a question of visibility but is also reinforced by audibility. Researches examining gender roles in adult interaction have shown how women play a supportive role in conversation, while men dominate, talking at greater length, and with greater frequency, interrupting women's contributions. Women who are successful in making equivalent and effective contributions in such interactions are then perceived by men as dominant, and women's talkativeness is measured against silence, not male talk. Women's talk is trivialised as 'gossip' or 'chit-chat', and topics of interest to women or initiated by women are taken over and reshaped to fit into male preferences (French and French, 1984; Spender, 1982; Jenkins and Kramarae, 1981).

The significance of such findings for teacher work and teacher development is considerable. Firstly, typical mixed-sex interaction operates in ways which convey an impression of male centrality and female marginality, thereby contributing to a general construction of greater male competence. Secondly, women teachers are likely to have greater possibilities of developing their ideas and gaining group endorsement for their priorities if interaction is more collaborative. However, mixed-sex interaction in schools is frequently not conducted in this way, especially in the more formal and most public occasions. Thirdly, effective female contributions are frequently appropriated by male members of a group, represented as male contributions, gaining group approval and credit for the individual concerned, whereas assertive female contributions are received often with indifference or with hostility. Fourthly, reputations for competence are very commonly built on public performance in staffroom interaction and the greater access and command of this that men teachers have as a group undoubtedly contributes to their individual credibility. Interestingly, women teachers often reject and refuse to engage in such public display, and insist on the priority of classroom work as the essential mark of competence. Thus through adult interaction, men teachers can display a kind of superficial authority, although this may not in any significant way enhance task performance, or the quality of learning and development of any of the participants in such interaction.

The nature of adult talk provides men teachers with many opportunities for excluding women from professional discussions and decision-making, and so simultaneously confirming male competence. The difficulties for women in re-orienting interactions to include them amount to more than a lack of assertiveness – they reflect the active role of male participants in controlling and shaping teacher talk. Moreover, part of the normality of mixed-sex interaction includes frequent reference to sexuality, which serves as a further curb on women's participation. At one level this can take the form of sexist comments which women can find patronising and offensive. More seriously it can take the form of sexual harassment by male teachers and pupils, and this intrudes into women teachers' sense of ease and safety in school.

Sexual harassment of girl pupils in schools has been a matter of considerable concern to some women educationalists, and researchers have identified the serious educational and social consequences of this for girls, and also for boys. Pat Mahony (1985) has emphasised how sexual harassment is part of a process of male learning of masculinity by boy pupils in which girls are objectified, and become the focus of fixation and conquest. Research and teacher experience also shows how men teachers react aggressively and with hostility when these issues are raised as a matter of concern. Girl pupil's complaints instead of producing disciplinary action often lead to the complainant being regarded as promiscuous and the cause of the acts of harassment, rather than the victim. Thus, the effects of such harassment are trivialised or denied, and the boys' behaviour effectively condoned – 'boys will be boys'.

The continuity of experience and reactions to sexual harassment for girls and women teachers is remarkable, and for women teachers, the consequences of complaining are similar. Anecdotal evidence suggests that sexual harassment is a common feature of school staffroom life and indeed, of female staff encounters with male outsiders, such as parents, and other visitors on the school premises. Research in progress at the time of writing with a survey of teachers and personal interview data indicates that the problem is pervasive, and a taken for granted part of many women teachers' experience.[6]

Although this kind of harassment, whether acts of actual physical assault, or other kinds of unwelcome behaviour of a sexual nature is commonplace, complaints are not. The reasons women have for not coming forward are an indicator of its effects on professional working relations, since women appear to fear victimisation, and not being believed, and suffer acute embarrassment. Moreover the formal response in education to complaints of this kind is to treat them as individual case work which increases the teacher's sense of being isolated and somehow carrying some responsibility for the offence.

Groups of women can be exposed to a level of harassment involving a number of staff in the same school, and still feel powerless to act, and the kind of working environment generated by this is one which is threatening, hostile and offensive. What is also in question for the victim is also the value of their work:

I had a headmaster who if I walked down a corridor . . . we had long corridors in the school, he would look at me as we were coming towards each other to talk to each other, and his eyes would be on my chest all the time. As I walked towards him whatever I was talking about and it wasn't just me . . . it was anybody who was well-endowed – he'd be talking to me and staring at my bosom whatever I was talking about . . . two men teachers said 'we knew you were going to get the job', and I said 'why?' and they said, 'well, he always appoints people with big tits', as they put it. You could imagine how I felt about that – my immediate thought was what does it matter that I'm any good as a teacher or – you know – sort of in my job, that's the only qualification that I *had* to have to get a job here in this school (woman headteacher, primary school).

Although sexual harassment can be manifested in grossly offensive acts, other incidents can be equally distressing and unacceptable to women but be seen by some men teachers as normal and acceptable in school working relationships:

Male teachers at a Birmingham school angered their women colleagues when they put up a girlie calendar in the staffroom. The National Union of Teachers conference at Scarborough heard the calendar showed naked women doing the housework and had the caption 'Women should stay at home'. (*Birmingham Evening Mail*, 11 April 1985)

The sexual harassment of women teachers by male colleagues is the most overt expression of a masculine presence and dominance in the school as a workplace. It is a kind of behaviour which is totally at variance with the context, that is, one of employment and co-working, relying on the collective exercise of expertise and skills of women and men teachers. The unacceptability of these behaviours can be remarked on in any environment but their complete inappropriateness in a workplace points to the role of sexual harassment as a form of male control, as Ann Oakley has expressed it, a sanction of a dominant group keeping its subordinates in line'. Emphasis on male and female sexuality in the flow of working interaction evokes male–female relations external to working relations and this serves as a further means of denying women a professional sphere and authority. Thus, when men teachers evoke female sexuality, they are attempting to reassert and confirm for themselves the limitations to women teachers' competence as colleagues, and to reinforce the stereotyping and the sexist mythology surrounding women as workers with which this chapter began.

'Ain't I a woman?'[7]

Some of the issues raised in this chapter may for some groups of women be almost irrelevant, not because they do not perceive or experience sexism in work, but because their position in society carries other disadvantages which have pre-eminence for them. For black women teachers the experience of racism at work may be a far more grievous abuse and oppression than sexism. Women from minority ethnic groups enter work institutions with a variety of cultural experience and affiliations which differ from those of the majority white groups, and as a result, their experience of sexism in schools can be different from that of white women from the dominant culture, irrespective of the effects of racism.

Marginalisation is an experience common to many women teachers. Black women teachers, however, can be invisible not only to men teachers, but also to white women colleagues. Black women find themselves excluded and disregarded in matters of professional consultation, in the staffroom, in meetings. Their contributions are likely to be undervalued or ignored, and their opinions not sought even on issues relating to the needs of black pupils.

In the case of black women teachers from Asian backgrounds, the stereotyping of Asian women as passive and submissive reinforces this invisibility. While it is true that such characteristics could be said to be an ideal typification of women, they acquire new force as a sterotype in the case of Asian teachers, and as a consequence become a justification for patronising and dismissive treatment from white colleagues. If, for example, an Asian woman teacher is sexually harassed by pupils, this can be interpreted as demonstrating her unsuitability for employment in teaching because of a lack of cultural 'fit'. If she rejects male teachers' physical contact, she is the victim of her own culture. If she behaves assertively, she is viewed with antagonism because she contradicts not so much a sexist stereotype, but a racist stereotype held about Asian women which predicts deference and compliance.

The pervasive emphasis on sexuality in our schools as in British society generally results in the operation of particular preconceptions of black women derived from a history of 'race' thinking about black people's sexuality so that Asian women teachers are seen as the victims of Asian male exploitation while Afro-Caribbean women are defined in terms of fecundity or promiscuity (Foster, 1985).

The experience of black women teachers is frequently one in which competence is viewed as circumscribed because of the operation of racist stereotypes and expectations by white colleagues. The relatively small numbers of black teachers results in their isolation, and a lack of professional support. Racial harassment in schools and the absence of adequate codes of practice to deal with this means that black teachers are left to cope with the stresses that this brings rather than being able to draw on the assistance of other teachers as would normally be the case. This experience therefore is a reminder of how positive action on women's issues may have little relevance for some groups of women, if it is forgotten that their needs as women may be embedded in other kinds of inequality and discrimination.

The images of women and men teachers' working relations presented here have been constructed primarily around women's perceptions and experience. These are derived from women teachers' own exploration of their work and gender roles in teaching, through women's training and other professional development activities, and through interview and research. The kinds of issues women raise and the connections made between work and women's roles in society more generally are noticeably absent from professional debate in education, despite their relevance for effective working and teacher development. This in itself is an indicator of the extent to which male perceptions and priorities determine educational discussion and teacher development.

The readiness of women teachers to engage in exploration and examination of gender identity and work, with a high degree of personal disclosure make it possible to develop a framework for action. However, the reluctance or inability of men teachers to undertake the same kind of exploration and personal disclosure limits what can be said here about men teachers' perceptions.

It is likely that for some men teachers the heterosexual norms of complementary male and female roles and characteristics, and male domination, are found oppressive. The emphasis in schools on a 'masculine' culture of aggressive physical presence, male self-certainty, self-advancement, and stereotyped career models can be as limiting for man a for women. It is certain that there are men teachers whose aspirations and behaviours are inhibited by the gender norms prevailing in teacher employment. Moreover, for men and women teachers, whether single, or childless, and especially for lesbian and gay colleagues, the prevailing definitions of heterosexuality and family lifestyle can limit the contribution and development of these particular groups and shape negatively others' views of their competence.

'The big buzz'[8]

Equal opportunities and gender issues in schools have tended to be perceived as problematic and as a matter about and for women and girls. However, such an approach ignores the context of women's work and lives, and the organisational structures within which they have to teach. Positive action training for women teachers needs to be located in a broad programme of institutional change and responsibility for this lies with employers and managers, first and foremost, rather than with women themselves.

Thus any positive action intervention needs a simultaneous strategy for changing the structures of employment and teacher attitude and behaviour, with curriculum development as an integral part of this. Training for women would be weakened in its benefits if not accompanied by organisational changes which acknowledge the effects of sex-stereotyping on, for example, selection and interviewing procedures, career development and career counselling and teacher interaction. Structures need to reflect the reality of women's lives at present while seeking to promote more flexible opportunities for women and men to enable them to follow employment patterns which accommodate family and other personal commitments and different lifestyles.

Priorities should be ensuring attitudinal change towards women and men's roles and encouraging a breakdown in the traditional division of labour occurring in schools, ending the role asymmetry discussed earlier in the chapter. Those in leadership positions have a particular duty to ensure the development and implementation of codes of practice on equitable selection and promotion procedures, and on sexual harassment, and equally so, on racial harassment. Headteachers have a central role in shifting the culture and kinds of interaction in school among staff towards a more positive and rewarding environment for women teachers and girls, and to signal the unacceptability of sexist practices through example, influence, and training.

Women teachers themselves have taken considerable steps to promote and develop positive action training in the face of apathy or outright hostility on the part of employers and colleagues. Typically, these have originated from an awareness of discrimination against women and their disadvantaged position in teaching career structures, while recognising characteristics in women's views of themselves which could limit career and professional development. In some instances, concern with career inequality has resulted in an emphasis on securing women in management. In others, the concern is for a broader target group. Although these have led to different providers and different provision, for example, by advisors, or advisory teachers, for LEA women teachers as in Enfield and Sheffield; by the NUT for union members; by a women teachers' group for other women teachers, there appears to be much in common about the nature and outcomes of these kinds of course.

One example is provided here by the Birmingham Women in Education Group which originated from a small group of women teachers seeking to support teacher debate on gender issues in curriculum and employment. At an early stage of the group's life, the need for women's training was felt sufficiently important for a group to form for the purpose of designing and delivering a women teacher's career and professional development course open to all women teachers in the City of Birmingham.

As in other instances of this kind of initiative, this very successful and popular course was a self-starting venture drawing on support outside the LEA, with a grant from the EOC, and advice from sympathetic outsiders. The course planners who were also the tutors were teachers working in their own time to plan and carry through a six-session course without fees, thus in one sense feeding a view of women's training as an 'extra', rather than an essential part of a professional development programme.

The pilot course established a pattern of co-tutoring and built in training of trainers, networking and mutual support for women in the group and later for those on the course in developing training skills. The methodology and content reflected the outward-looking stance of women in this area of training, seeking contacts and advice from outside education, from individuals or groups with experience in the field.

In successive years, the course has been built around assumptions about women's training needs, which were confirmed by women participants' requests and responses. These ideas have reflected much of the discussion earlier in the chapter and focused on a range of topics which it was felt would be valuable and significant for women as a group. These have included an appreciation of women's situation and experience in the school system, and of sexism; recognising and voicing this, and attempting to see this as valid rather than devaluing this; assessing and asserting the professional contribution women teachers make in their individual situations; examining women's various roles at home and school; considering career and professional roles at home and school; working on specific topics of interest such as applications for posts and interview practice; assertiveness training, and dealing with aggressive and sexist behaviour from colleagues.

The experience of such courses seems to follow similar patterns irrespective of who the providers are – advisor, teacher, teacher union organisers. Firstly, they appeal to a wide variety of women at different stages of life and career, and with different perspectives on their experience as teachers and women – it seems that there is a common core of experience and concern that women's training can respond to. Secondly, women are especially responsive to the all-women environment despite initial anxiety for some in being in such a situation. This is experienced as supportive and non-threatening, and encouraging a high level of activity and commitment. Thirdly, the exploration of personal and professional experience, perceptions and values, which is usually part of such training, is felt appropriate and worthwhile. For some women it can be the first opportunity to examine sources of conflict in professional and personal life, especially if the school is felt to be unsympathetic or unsatisfactory as a workplace for women. Fourthly, women teachers, irrespective of status, reveal the considerable pressures generated through sex stereotyping and male attitudes, and the negative consequences for their work, but find the courses both a relief and a source of confidence building. Fifth, such courses seem to produce a strong commitment to action, and empowerment. The strong desire to promote action not only of benefit to the individual but to colleagues and pupils in school is a marked feature of participants' responses to such training. Sixth, women teachers comment favourably on the highly effective collaborative working style of these courses which is often felt to be difficult in male dominated work places.

Training for women teachers is not a solution in itself to the disadvantage women experience. In the case of black women, some of whom have been course participants and tutors, such training can be of value but in view of the particular position of black teachers, other kinds of training interventions dealing also with racism are needed, and for some black women separate black women's groupings may be vital for additional support. Training is in any case one means among a variety of strategies for positive action aimed at effecting organisational change.

However, women teachers' training has demonstrated how women seeking to change their situation, can take the initiative, and amply demonstrate their ability to work together for improvements in the education service which will benefit teachers and pupils. It also provides a powerful example of how women teachers have strengths for action and organisation which are under-utilised and undervalued in schools. Women of all kinds of personal and professional histories, in different parts of the country, have revealed energy and commitment to their work but anger about their treatment. This reaction to women's training is testimony to the waste and abuse of women teachers' talent and experience in the education service as it is currently organised and led. It is this problem that positive action is intended to affect and change, in the interests of enhancing the life of our schools.

Notes

1. See for example, some of the teachers' views affirming this point of view in the Clwyd survey (Clwyd/EOC, 1983).
2. Reason given by a male interviewer to a female candidate for not appointing her to the post of Head of Music Department.
3. Ann Oakley, 1981.
4. This has also been apparent in initial interview work conducted in research into teachers' careers. Personal communication, Ann Kindleyside.
5. Dante, *Purgatorio*, Canto XXV:47.
6. This research originated out of the School Management Development and Women Teachers Project. It is now being conducted jointly by the NUT, NAS/UWT and NATFHE.
7. Bel Hooks.
8. Woman teacher describing her experience of being tutor and participant in women's training.

5

The ivory tower:
positive action for women
in higher education

JANETTE WEBB

> The University is above all a hierarchy. At the top is a small cluster of highly paid and prestigious persons, chiefly men, whose careers entail the services of a very large base of ill-paid or unpaid persons, chiefly women: wives, research assistants, secretaries, teaching assistants, cleaning women, waitresses in the faculty club, lower echelon administrators and women students who are used in various ways to gratify the male ego. . . . Each women in the University is defined by her relationship to the men in power instead of her relationship to other women up and down the scale. (Adrienne Rich, 1979, p. 136)

Women in higher education: segregated labour and segregated courses

The government and direction of higher education in the UK remains largely, as the above quotation indicates, under the control of white middle-class men. Despite the 1960s' and 1970s' expansion in jobs and student places, and the accompanying commitment by government and institutions to equal access and equal opportunity, higher education remains extremely divided in terms of men and women, black and white, young and old and social class (see Finch and Rustin, 1986).

As in other public employment spheres, women's jobs in higher education reflect the division of labour in the domestic sphere: women do the service and support work – catering, cleaning, secretarial and clerical – while men do the professional, administrative and technical work. The sexual divide is marked also within staff grades: in terms of weekly-paid staff women do the cleaning and catering while men have the portering, maintenance and security jobs. Segregation is also notable within job hierarchies. Those women who have jobs in the professional, administrative and technical grades have a disproportionate share of the low-level research and teaching assistant or basic grade library and administrative jobs. Despite equivalent qualifications and track records, they ironically fare worse, in terms of the share of professional jobs, in those disciplines with higher numbers of women students (Blackstone and Fulton, 1974). Even in the secretarial and clerical area, women staff have not gained as good access to the highest graded jobs as the few men in these grades. The conventional employment practices of institutions of higher education result in men (and not women) getting the best jobs whatever their numbers.

The 1960s and 1970s expansion of higher education was presented as a means of enabling increased access for all those with the required level of ability (typically measured in terms of 'A' levels) who wanted higher education, while maintaining academic standards. Thus notions of equality centred on access to higher education and on the opening of degree qualifications to children of working-class parents. The suitability of current standards, set largely by the existing practitioners in the various disciplines, to the interests and priorities of different groups (such as women) remained unexamined. Access was also talked about in terms of individual merit or ability: the idea that such essential, individualised ability exists in measurable form and is reflected in examination performance may have been used strategically as a means of breaking traditional 'grace and favour' arrangements, and may have been sincerely believed in as a means of promoting fairer treatment. Unfortunately, if white men (and some women) from middle-class backgrounds are the chief beneficiaries of the assessment system, supposedly meritocratic judgements are also a convenient means of legitimating the exclusion of everyone else. Hence there are those who believe that the system already reflects the distribution of 'ability' in the population: apparently it is concentrated in the white, middle-class male.

What then, were the effects of access of the 1960s–1970s growth in universities, colleges and polytechnics? Despite an annual rate in the 1960s of about 8 per cent and a steady expansion in numbers in the 1970s, Williamson (1986) states that much has remained the same, even though the packaging is different. Thus, for instance, between 1961 and 1977 the Age Participation Rate (the number of young entrants into higher education as a proportion of the relevant 18 year old age group) increased from 7.5 per cent to 12.7 per cent (Williamson, 1986, p. 72). Students entering university continue, however, to be drawn heavily from the higher socio-economic groups. The Robbins principle of 1963 that all those qualified and seeking places in higher education should have access has, in its particular form of operation, served to reinforce the previous inequalities.

This generalisation holds not just in terms of social class, but also for women, black and older people. The percentage of women students in universities has increased from 29.2 per cent in 1956 to 38.4 per cent in 1981–2 (University Statistical Record cited in Williamson, 1986). However, the increased numbers of women students have come mainly from middle-class backgrounds so that whilst the overall proportion of women has increased, the proportion entering university from a working-class background has declined slightly.

There is some evidence that women overseas students receive worse treatment at many levels than men overseas students. Goldsmith and Shawcross (1985), using statistics from the British Council and questionnaire and interview responses from the women, demonstrated that women are disadvantaged and discriminated against not only in terms of numbers selected, but also in terms of clustering on 'low status' courses which lead to low status jobs at home; they have not gained increased representation in the 1975–1985 United Nations decade for women and women received less than one quarter of the available scholarships. They also face particular problems of social isolation, since they are not allowed to bring their spouse and children and often cannot go alone to bars and student dining rooms. They experience a combination of racial and sexual harrassment from staff and students.

As is now well-documented, women undergraduates are concentrated in the social sciences, humanities and life sciences; very few women study engineering and technology (see *University Statistical Record, 1982–3* vol. 1, Students and Staff). There is also some anecdotal evidence of segregation *within* degree courses in social sciences, such that women are clustered into those aspects traditionally regarded as humanistic (e.g. personnel management in business studies courses; child development or clinical options in psychology courses) while men are clustered on the 'social theory', 'ergonomics', 'production management' and related options traditionally regarded as 'hard-edged' or concerned with the manipulation of the environment.

In terms of university degree performance, overall men get more firsts and more third-class honours degrees than women. Broadly, two types of explanation are used to account for such differences in performance: one is biological (women are regarded as naturally lacking in intellectual qualities which some men have), the other is social (conventional assessments of ability are made by men, the curriculum is dominated by male interests and male definitions of important or valuable knowledge; thus women's interests, experience, modes of expression and learning are excluded or under-represented and under-valued).

The biological explanation of differences in performance is still publicly adhered to despite well-researched studies which show that variation in scoring on tests of ability owes much to differences in test construction, administration, population sampling, statistical tests of significant differences and so on (see Rose, 1985; Anastasi, 1958). There is also some research which indicates that women's academic work is rated lower than men's by external examiners, but not by internal examiners who know the students (Bradley, 1985).

This male belief in women's inferiority, combined with the insecurity of the same men over their own status and ability, remains an important influence over the continuing exclusion of women from significant jobs in higher education. One consequence of the tendency to legitimate social inequality in terms of a supposed deficiency in women is that policies which regard 'equal opportunities' as equivalent to equal access to jobs and courses based on 'free competition between individuals', important though they are, are insufficient.

The limitations of an 'access approach' lie in a number of directions. First it fails to address practices, standards and curricula within institutions. Second, it fails to deal proactively with existing segregation of courses into 'men's subjects' and 'women's subjects'. Third, the concentration on judgements of individual merit, based increasingly on 'A' level grades or formal qualification, serves to legitimate the *status quo*: if you failed to get the job or a place on the course, it must be your personal lack of ability. Fourth, women are at a disadvantage if they step out of the qualifications and achievement race to raise children (such experience is geneally regarded as irrelevant to suitability for jobs or courses). The policy generally benefits the white middle-class population who typically have considerable informal knowledge about how to 'manipulate the system': which courses are worth doing, which departments are most enterprising or attract research grants, and which degree courses guarantee good jobs.

If there has to be competition for places, and the criterion for selection is ability, women's organisations have to challenge the increasingly narrow unitary concept of 'ability' as equated with formal qualifications. The exclusion of other indicators of relevant experience results in the exclusion of many able women. Related to this is the need to provide for greater diversity of curricula and courses within and between institutions, in order to facilitate the representation of women staff and students across a wide range of departments and courses, including those in science and engineering.

Strategies for change

The structural divisions and inequalities between women and men in higher education may be relatively well-documented, but the routes to effective change are less clear. Two approaches to the problem are currently discernible: the equal opportunities model and a more critical, transformative approach. In the UK elements of both tend to be used simultaneously. They are not, in a straightforward sense, in conflict, although it is important to distinguish between them and to be aware of their strengths and limitations. In the end, what is achieved through their use is likely to be dependent on political intentions behind the plans, as well as the resourcing and organisation of the work.

Most British and North American policies are based on an EO model which tends to be interpreted as equal rights with a white man. The UK sex and race discrimination laws are based on this principle. An example of the broad approach is the recent campaign to increase the number of girls holding engineering apprenticeships. Male norms and values and ways of working remain largely unchallenged: the 'girls' have to learn to be like the 'boys', even when they are treated by the boys with disinterest at best and derision at worst.

The transformative approach, in contrast, is concerned with developing critiques of the status quo, its values, established forms of authority and traditional notions of 'ability' or 'career' or 'full-time job', which effectively exclude most women, or offer them employment solely on male terms (for example Cockburn, 1983a; Jewson and Mason, 1986). Criticisms have centred on issues such as 'normal' linear career patterns, requiring full-time paid work and the servicing of a 'wife', definitions of meritocratic performance in terms of research and publication in the established disciplinary traditions and grading systems which stop secretarial and clerical staff being regarded as suitable applicants for administrative posts. A significant body of feminist research has questioned the exclusion of women from social, historical, economic, political, scientific, technological and every other type of analysis (Acker, 1980; Spender, 1982; Cockburn, 1983b; Merchant, 1982; Keller, 1983; Harding and Hintikka, 1983; Evans *et al.*, 1986).

The case studies: America and Britain

If you want to discover the benefits of positive action then just follow this simple programme. (EOC, 1982)

Although available feminist critiques are wide-ranging and increasingly sophisticated, their development into strategies for change is limited. Meanwhile despite opposition, EO policies are becoming more common. Sociological analysis of such policies has also highlighted their limited impact on the redistribution of jobs (see, for example, Salaman, 1986; Jewson and Mason, 1986; Jenkins, 1986; Robbins, 1986). The criticisms have centred on the problems of implementing the formal, standardised procedures supposed to be necessary for equal opportunity, and the fact that the structure of job hierarchies, training and promotion routes remain unaffected. Previously there has been almost a conspiracy of silence over discussion of the process by which equal opportunities policies are introduced and how their effectiveness should be evaluated.

The assumption made by public bodies who advise on how to introduce and implement an EO policy is that the process is straightforward, progresses logically step-by-step with minimum disruption, hostility or conflict and has obvious economic benefits to employers. The experience of trying to create and implement even relatively minor changes in fact seems to be totally the opposite: the EO model, based on attempts to formalise employment practices, is often regarded with incomprehension or unwillingness, accompanied by (more or less) defensive assertions that no one is discriminated against here anyway (see, for example, Robbins, 1986).

Introducing EO policies is a highly political process, which requires sustained commitment, continuing re-appraisal over long periods (it is *not* a 'once-only' intervention) and considerable labour and investment of resources. If it is successful, it disrupts the status quo and upsets vested interests, engenders considerable hostility from different groups and typically the demonstration of obvious economic benefits to employers is difficult to show, although employers may be pleased with resulting improvements in women's morale and quality of work. Thus only those employers who are, or can be made to be, in some sense publicly accountable are likely to demonstrate any commitment to such changes. This is acknowledged more explicitly in the USA, where federal and state legislation requires firms in receipt of loans, grants or contracts from government, to adopt and comply with affirmative action guidelines which emphasise the recruitment, training and promotion of women and ethnic minority groups in areas and grades where they are under-represented in the labour force. This is known as contract compliance. Federal and state agents evaluate the efforts of the institution on an annual basis, and further contracts are contingent upon a demonstration of compliance and reasonable effort to meet recruitment and promotion targets. The organisation of affirmative action is thus top-down, with an explicit financial motive to comply. In Britain, the legislation is passive: there is a requirement not to discriminate against individuals, but no requirement to take positive action. Employers are therefore inclined to act in the interests of previously excluded groups, only in the face of external or internal political or moral pressure or economic sanctions or because they have a publicly declared commitment to social equality (such as in institutions of higher education and even here, there are widely varying opinions on what constitutes social equality).

The intention here is to describe two case studies of social intervention in order to explore the difficulties of devising and implementing equal opportunities policies for higher education and to analyse future prospects. The first case study is based on the Affirmative Action Programme of a major US state university. As well as demonstrating the methods of managing such a programme, the aim is to show the limits of the equal rights approach. The second case study is based on a Positive Action Project undertaken at a technological university in England: strategies combining 'equal rights' and 'transformative'-type campaigning were developed by a women's staff group at local level. The difficulties and limitations of such a grass-roots approach are discussed.

1. *Affirmative action in a North American state university*

North American state universities are regarded as having set the standards for equality of opportunity in US employment: they have responded in an organised and efficient manner to state and federal legislation which requires employers in receipt of public funds 'to make additional efforts to recruit, employ and promote qualified members of groups formerly excluded, even if that exclusion cannot be traced to particular discriminatory action on the part of the employer'.

In the particular university studied, the director of Affirmative Action described the establishment of the programme as having taken place almost overnight, as a result of threats, issued by the federal goverment, to withdraw financial support unless the university could demonstrate its commitment to a deliberate affirmative action policy. The post of director of the programme was created during that summer; it is a position with impressive authority, for those of us used to under-funded, marginalised women's groups.

The central office was located in a main campus administration building, close to the university president. Hence the director reports to the president and works from the office of the president. The Affirmative Action office has wide-ranging responsibility for the development of the programme and the monitoring and recording of university employment patterns. The recurring emphasis is on increasing the numbers of ethnic minorities and women in jobs and grades in the employment hierarchy where they are traditionally absent or under-represented. The university must demonstrate to government officials that they are genuinely working to implement goals and hence must provide detailed annual audit reports on staff numbers in all grades according to sex and ethnicity.

Apart from the production of the annual audit, the office has to set goals and timetables for recruitment, by collecting and maintaining current statistics on the structure of the labour market in each area of university employment. For example, a final recruitment goal is set when the actual number of female or ethnic minority staff in a job group, in a department, section or unit, is lower than the number that could be anticipated, given the numbers of ethnic minorities or women available in the relevant labour pool. 'Good faith' hiring efforts are made to recruit the specified numbers of women or ethnic minorities. The final goal is not, however, a quota but represents the 'under-utilization' of women or minorities in a job group. Seven broad job categories, devised by the US government for the analysis of employment in higher education, are used to define the relevant job groups. These categories are:

1. Executive/administrative/managerial
2. Faculty
3. Professional non-faculty
4. Clerical/secretarial
5. Technical/paraprofessional
6. Skilled crafts
7. Service maintenance

The *availability* of women and ethnic minorities amongst

teaching/instructional staff is estimated in terms of percentages in the national pool of potential applicants for a given discipline (for example, based on the number of black Americans graduating with PhDs in electrical engineering in the appropriate year, and so on). The availability of women and ethnic minorities amongst non-teaching staff is estimated in terms of percentage in the appropriate (local, regional or national) pool of potential applicants for a typical job. The data used are a combination of such factors as the present numbers of women and ethnic minorities available for promotion into a job group and women and ethnic minorities graduating from college or vocational courses and US census data.

Any department or section which has a final goal for recruitment is not necessarily expected to meet the goal in the coming year, or as job opportunities arise. Instead, timetables are set which estimate the expected number of years needed to meet a final goal, taking account of the rate of labour turnover. On the basis of this timetable, an annual goal is set, according to the number of placements expected in the coming year which could be used to meet the final goal in any job group.

Procedures for recruitment and promotion　Monitoring the implementation of such a programme requires careful accounting, checking of detail, maintaining accurate records of staff turnover, as well as the collection of data concerning appropriate labour pools. The workforce of US universities is very large by UK standards; in this case, it was slightly less than 11000.

The AA office focuses on three types of 'event': hiring, promotion and 'terminations' (which may be either a resignation or the end of a contract). In the recruitment area, this includes the occurrence of vacancies, the applications received, short-list drawn up, appointment made and written reasons why any women or ethnic minority applicants were excluded from the shortlist or not appointed after interview. At the end of each academic year, assessments are matched against goals to check for 'successes' and 'failures'. In the promotion area, applications are monitored along with actual promotions and awards of tenure for teaching staff. Reasons for leaving are monitored and distribution of people by age, sex and ethnic group, placed on 'reduction in force' status (that is, made redundant or redeployed) are checked. The data suggest changes in the work force which are selectively followed up by further investigation: for example, a pilot cohort study of men and women academics was conducted to establish reasons for smaller proportions of women gaining promotion. While staff from ethnic minority backgrounds were as successful in gaining promotion as white men, women were not (12.5 per cent of the women were promoted, compared with 42.9 per cent of the men). Main findings were that women tended to publish less, on average, than men. Some of the reasons for this were that women seemed to co-author articles with senior faculty less frequently than men (25 per cent of women had co-authored articles, compared with 52.3 per cent of their male peers). Collaboration with senior colleagues was found to be an important predictor of promotion: 61.3 per cent of those who worked with senior colleagues were promoted, compared to only 12.5 per cent of those who did not.

Needless to say, the implementation of such a wide range of monitoring activity, combined with selective investigations, was received with varying degrees of enthusiasm across the university, with some staff suggesting that you could only make appointments or give financial assistance for research if you had a black, female, physically disabled applicant, hence meeting all annual goals at once. . . . Conversely, the 'old boy' networks still seemed to be thriving in the faculty club.

Diffusion and implementation   The extent to which the programme makes the university an institution which is less socially divided according to gender and ethnicity and more egalitarian and open to the influence of women and ethnic minorities depends on creating a reasonable degree of awareness of its existence, understanding of its purposes and willingness to act on its principles routinely, by staff across the university. American universities, even though closer to the executive decision-making model than the UK universities, are relatively decentralised. Consequently, the affirmative active office has to be able to influence the activities of 'hiring, firing and promoting', while not being directly responsible for any of these decisions.

The main ways by which this is set in motion are through the central visibility of the office, with a director who is executive assistant to the president; through the seven office staff who work either in implementing particular programmes (such as for women, ethnic minorities, handicapped and elderly, and for ethnic minority students), or in collection and analysis of data; and through the university's affirmative action co-ordinators who are selected from each part of the university to provide information and oversee the AA activities in their areas. The AA office also works closely with the personnel office to review staffing policies. A number of advisory and constituent groups provide feedback on the implementation and direction of the programme.

Apart from providing an institutional focus for the network of interest groups and publicising its activities and commitments via departmental co-ordinators, the AA office is also the centre for counselling and management of grievance procedure for those who feel they have been discriminated against. Consequently, not only is it in contact with new grievances, it is also an important location where the definition of discriminatory treatment is managed: it would perhaps be revealing to conduct an analysis of how such complaints are dealt with.

Lastly, an important means of influence and awareness raising was via a training package, including video and written materials, to make sexual harassement unacceptable in the University. The video was scripted and directed by the Women's Network and the AA office and used as a vehicle for explaining women's understanding of what constitutes harassment. The training package was used with groups of men and women who worked together in particular departments, as well as other interested groups and had been sold for use by other North American colleges.

Results. Despite a highly-organised, well-resourced and diverse approach to the affirmative action policy (and the coviction of some administrators that the university was being changed to a hotbed of black and feminist radicalism), any movement in overall proportions of men and women, and black and white, across jobs and grades, was slow. The university's affirmative action programmes had been in existence since 1980: between 1980 and 1983 the workforce had declined by approximately 6 per cent to slightly less than 11000. Whilst the overall percentage of ethnic minorities increased slightly from 11 per cent to 11.8 per cent, their numbers did not actually change and the percentage in the executive, administrative and managerial group declined from 6.9 per cent to

5.5 per cent. The number of women employed declined over the same period, but remained at around 50 per cent of the total workforce. The numbers of women in the administrative groups increased slightly (from 17.5 per cent to 20.9 per cent). Asian people were the only group whose numbers increased in tenured or tenure-track academic posts (3.6 per cent to 4.8 per cent). The number of women academics fell, although their percentage remained the same at around 17 per cent. Out of 201 tenure-track appointments made during 1983, 29.4 per cent were women and 12.4 per cent were from the ethnic minority groups. The majority of women and ethnic minorities were appointed at the lowest level of 'instructor'.

Between 1980 and 1984 the distribution of women in the main occupational groups remained broadly similar. In particular, there was still a high degree of segregation between secretarial/clerical jobs and managerial/administrative grades. Women continue to occupy approximately half the 'professional non-faculty' technical and paraprofessional jobs but only 19.5 per cent of faculty posts. The optimistic news was that between 1980 and 1984, women became more evenly distributed across faculty ranks. The largest proportion in both 1980 and 1984 were at the assistant professor rank (37.5 per cent of women in 1984) while the largest proportion of men were full professors (53 per cent of all men 1984). In 1984 there were 71 women professors out of 1112 (that is, 6.4 per cent). They are not, however, evenly distributed across subjects and departments, but are concentrated in the conventionally 'female' areas of library service, nursing, education and social work. An examination of numbers of posts lost of gained between 1980 and 1984 also reveals that these areas where women are most concentrated have been cut back most significantly.

Limitations of the affirmative action approach. A well-resourced and efficiently administered policy does not therefore guarantee significant changes in the distribution of jobs between men and women in the work force; such changes are slow and benefits to women and ethnic minorities hard to win and likely to vanish without the continuing work of an affirmative action office. The case study demonstrates the complexity of monitoring and implementing policy, even in an organisation which makes public commitment to its aims.

The programme was operating during a period of overall reductions in the work force; hence new appointments are relatively few and goals were met frequently as a result of staff leaving or being moved to a different department, rather than because of new appointments: access to the 'good jobs' is slow. The major difficulty with the overall approach is the underlying assumption that the pre-existing institutional divisions between jobs and grades are equally acceptable to men and women, black and white: the terms of success and failure are once again set by the dominant groups and their conventions. Hence occupational segregation is likely to be maintained, unless women are willing and able to work on men's terms or unless, for example, the conventional image of clerical and secretarial work is upgraded. In this case, women still tended to be concentrated in the service-orientated jobs with effectively a barrier between clerical and administrative grades. Women in the academic-career grades still found it harder than men to apply successfully for tenure or promotion to professor: they published less, presumably they still had a greater share of child-care, perhaps they were not as keen as the men to be caught up in the powerful achievement ethos of the USA and possibly they were not 'taken up' be senior staff as readily as their male colleagues.

The bureaucracy associated with maintaining employment practice and publicly accountable selection and promotion decisions engenders hostility in those administrators principally responsible for filling in the relevant forms. The goals of recruitment and promotion at the local department or unit level differed from those of the AA office: local recruiters, for example, aim to select the person they want for the job (according to a range of local, informal criteria related to the social acceptability of the applicant). Subsequently they aim to 'rationalise' the subjective preference according to the AA office's terms of individual public 'merits' such as qualifications, relevant experience, etc. Federal reporting and contract compliance requirements are also in an important sense double-edged. The setting of goals for recruitment cannot be a neutral process: ambitious goals look very bad for the university when they are not met. The threat of withdrawal of money has the effect of focusing activity on monitoring annual staff changes. This is an important part of evaluating change, but also makes issues of occupational segregation side-issues rather than a central focus: the AA policy serves an instrumental purpose for the university, by ensuring continued funding.

2. *A positive action project in a technological university*

Positive action in the UK is based on different principles from US affirmative action. It is generally defined as the development and implementation of equal opportunities policies, which can be wide-ranging or minimal. In common with other positive action projects in European organisations, the UK work began not from the issuing of a policy statement or equality clause, but from the mutual concerns of a small group of women trying to focus on one or two particular problem areas. Povall (1984) suggests that this starting point distinguishes the North American and the European approaches. The European practice probably reflects the lesser commitment at higher levels of the hierarchy and the absence of an explicit contract compliance clause from the European legislation.

The women most involved were junior staff, often with short contracts, and, inevitably, with little public authority or access to resources. The origin of the Women's Group was when the three women academics in the engineering faculty started to meet informally. Their initial work resulted in a report on the situation of women engineering students and the existence of a women's staff group was subsequently advertised in the university magazine. Other women, initially from the academic and administrative staff and research students, became involved. The common concern at this stage was with feelings of frustration, harassment and isolation, in the context of a technological university where all senior positions were held by men, engineering and physical science courses were dominated by men students, and most women staff were in service and support jobs, associated with low pay and poor status.

The group was a place to air grievances and to discover that what individuals had taken to be their personal 'failings' were generally shared in common. The major gains from this period were in personal confidence and friendship between women which crossed departmental and structural categories. An important side-effect of this was to create links between women staff which enabled a better understanding of the machinery of university decision-making and to act proactively as a pressure group for women's interests in the university; individuals participated more on university committees, such as Senate, Council and Faculty Boards and wrote articles for the campus magazine. Group meetings were never solely social, but involved reasonably systematic work on a current project. As a staff group, women involved were primarily interested in the detrimental effects on their working lives of the university as an employer. Consequently, pressure group activity focused on the work place but included its treatment of women students. It was not a specifically academic group, in the sense that meetings were not primarily concerned with developing feminist analyses or with women's studies, although those women who were teaching undergraduate and postgraduate courses, and/or doing research, were concerned with how to teach and how to write up their research from a perspective which treates gender relations as fundamental rather than as an afterthought.

One of the continuing concerns of women in meeting was that the university employed almost 50 per cent women staff, but mostly in 'invisible' jobs – cleaning, catering, secretarial and clerical work. While many may be in demanding, stressful and difficult jobs, their work was not typically recogniscd in such terms. Women in the academic and professional jobs were regarded as relatively privileged by other women. This was a source of tension throughout: the project tried to draw in women from across the 'structural boundaries' created by the university status hierarchy. It was, therefore, important to examine first the institution as an employer of women.

Work on the position of women students focused on their distribution in science and engineering, provision for them in terms of careers advice and general counselling and the university's description of itself and its courses in the prospectus and by the schools liaison office. The group members were generally ambivalent about encouraging women students to study engineering and science: without significant commitments to new types of courses, new teaching methods and provision aimed at women, there are good reasons for women to opt for a course where there are already significant numbers of female students (see Cockburn, 1983b). Influence over curriculum development in such institutions requires, for example, concerted action through the University Senate and influence over heads of departments in science and engineering. It needs to be developed and led by women scientists and engineers. Yet these were the weakest areas where most women academic staff were few and far between.

The women's group activity therefore focused on issues which could be addressed, given numbers and distribution in particular departments and grades. The presentation of an opportunity to be project-oriented was significant: at an early stage, the vice chancellor introduced a university-wide 'Innovation Fund'. Some of the group members prepared an application for part of this money to employ a women's adviser. The university turned down the application on the grounds that the case for an adviser required further documentation. The work did, however, result in a university studentship for research into women and higher education.

The initial attempt to gain funding and a degree of public success (here was an *ad hoc* group being given university money) encouraged the group to continue to seek financial support, resulting in a successful application to the Equal Opportunities Commission for a grant to employ a co-ordinator to: 'direct and consolidate the activities of the women's staff group and ensure that the University is increasingly made aware of, and encouraged to act on, the present imbalance between women and men.'

Managing the project. The Positive Action Project had two broad aims, which were formulated by the women's group:

1. to ensure that women working and studying at the university have real access to the full range of courses and jobs and have the opportunity to progress to other areas of work and study.
2. to ensure that women in the university encounter a supportive atmosphere, where conditions of work are compatible with personal responsibilities, where there are facilities for women and courses are carefully designed and run, bearing in mind that they are for women as well as for men.

Much of the work of the first few months centred on trying to devise an appropriate and acceptable form of management for the project: central problems concerned how to develop a reasonable, trusting relationship between the voluntary group and the paid co-ordinator, and how to make the general, long-term aims of the group concrete and amenable to translation into short-term activities. The formal structure eventually relied on consisted of a women's action committee, with members draw from across the widest possible range of women's jobs, and a series of related working parties who took responsibility for developing particular campaigns. The committee aimed to oversee the balance and timing of activities and to work with the co-ordinator to direct the project. It was also a forum for more exploratory discussion of issues relating to equal opportunity. Minutes of meeting were taken in turn by members and used as a means of checking progress from week to week. These meetings were rarely easy; 'equal opportunity' has different meanings depending on the person's position in the jobs hierarchy, as well as their political, feminist or trade union views, and is influenced by pragmatic assessments of what might be achieved, given the financial constraints, cuts in higher education, the degree of commitment of the principal university officers and the time, energy and conviction of the women.

Areas of work. The creation of a statistical staff profile demonstrated the expected pattern of job segregation, with women staff concentrated in service and support jobs. There were no women professors or senior administrators, although a small number of women occupy key posts such as directors of library and information services, career services and tutored video instruction. There was, however, only one remaining woman academic in the engineering faculty. Women occupied a disproportionate share of low-graded jobs within each group, progressed more slowly than men with similar lengths of service and had a disproportionate share of short-term contracts.

Raising awareness of the project with women throughout the university (as well as male university officers) was carried out principally by publicity campaigns and repeated workplace meetings with women staff in different departments and grades. The main source of publicity centred on the production of a monthly broadsheet, distributed to all women staff via the internal mailing system (this was not a popular development with the male post-room staff). The issues identified at these meetings together with the women's group discussions and priorities of the action committee formed the focus for working parties in the areas of staff development, flexible working hours and, on the student side, women in science and engineering. Workplace meetings revealed, across most groups of staff, general dissatisfaction or frustrations about the failure of the institution to provide training and opportunities for promotion between grades and job categories. Cleaning staff were not encouraged or provided with training to improve their qualifications or prospects of movement into more skilled work. Secretarial and clerical staff were not given the opportunity to move into the portering jobs held by men. Catering staff were trapped by a fore shortened grading system and felt the lack of recognition of their administrative responsibilities: they were not generally considered suitable applicants for administrative posts. Academic and administrative staff were increasingly concerned about the concentration of women staff employed on short-term contracts, the accompanying breakdown of the 'age for wage' assumptions about pay, with little prospect of future improvement, as well as the operation of 'informal' age limits on recruitment which indirectly discriminate against women. The short-term response of the women's committee was at three levels: first, to submit proposals to the staff officer for 'good practice' training policy and, second, to make recommendations relating to advertisements for jobs, design of application forms and selection. These attentions were received with polite interest, a degree of support and good intentions, but few visible sustained changes in routine practices.

The project also investigated methods of opening more jobs to women on a flexible part-time or shared basis. Although the university personnel officer was not opposed to schemes such as job-sharing he would not actively promote them. The final working party concentrated on women students and was able to make changes to publicity, prospectuses and so on aimed at school-leavers, as well as influencing the careers service in terms of advice given to young women graduates looking for employment. All of this was highly acceptable within the University, because of the desire to attract well-qualified school-leavers. The contentious issues of curriculum were not, however, systematically addressed.

Results. The effectiveness of such campaigns is not shown in the statistics: most of the original women's group members have left the university. The subjective view of most women involved at the end of the co-ordinator's period of employment was that the project was not successful. Despite the efforts to manage and direct the work tightly, with short-term goals in mind, there were still no women professors, no publicised training policy and no men rushing to confess the errors of their chauvinistic ways. With hindsight however, these aims seem highly unrealistic: it is possible to see the benefits of the project; not, unfortunately, in numbers of women earning better pay and having better prospects, but in terms of other, qualitative indicators, which may eventually result in material benefits.

The most significant effects of the project were in terms of what is loosely called 'awareness'. First, women staff directly involved in some aspect of the work, regardless of their previous interest in women's employment and education, not only learned a great deal about the existing situation of women and the different ways of interpreting 'equal opportunities', but also became more aware of the strengths, skills and responsibilities of women staff, and their significant, if typically under-valued, part in the running of the University. Consequently, there were general improvements in confidence and public activity of women in the University. Conversely, men became more aware of women as a group with some common interests: there is informal evidence to indicate that there is less overt disparagement of women. Whatever the private views of some men, the issues of sexism have been raised publicly and challenged, in departmental meetings, faculty meetings, with personnel and training officers, in the students' guild, and so on. Structural inequalities and instances of sexist treatment undoubtedly remain, but the silence has been overcome. The value of women's networks should not be under-estimated: not only is women's sense of isolation overcome, the network indirectly influences men who are aware that it is the only forum which crosses the boundaries created by the institutional hierarchy. The greater awareness of women staff and students has resulted in a range of the group's concerns being taken up. These are, for example, improved publicity materials which show women doing a-typical work and which do not rely on the male term 'he' to 'encompass' the female 'she'. There is a woman doctor in the university health centre, and a woman counsellor operating a university wide service, with assertiveness courses on general offer. Proposals for training continue to be 'under review' (in the absence of a training officer), but a younger personnel officer introduced aspects of sexism awareness into standard interviewer training and initiated systematic induction for all new staff in clerical, secretarial and aministrative grades. Lastly the university is commencing an externally-conducted review of secretarial and clerical work, in the light of changes in office technology. To ensure representation of women's interests, the next stage of a positive action project would seem to necessitate the presentation to the University Council of a report with directed recommendations for action, concentrating on recruitment, training, promotion and grading, and highlighting those areas identified as particularly frustrating by groups of women staff.

It is also valuable to analyse the 'blocks' to more dramatic changes in opportunities for women during this period. The most important context was the financial one: severe cuts of 30 per cent in recurrent funding meant the loss of large numbers of academic and support staff jobs. Key posts, such as personnel and training officers, university medical officer, and senior academic and administrative positions remained vacant for long periods or have been permanently shelved; very few new appointments were made. The combination of threats to future employment and the introduction of a more centralised executive management style resulted in few women being willing to campaign for better opportunities: it seemed more important to hang on or, better still, find another job elsewhere, and depart with the 'mobility incentive' money. New appointments, invariably made on shorter – and shorter – term contracts discourage and disable continuing campaigns, by breaking continuity of women staff, who are not given time or opportunity to develop any general interest in the university. The advantages of crisis-change and upheaval are in the breaking-down of past traditions, but considerable commitment is needed by senior male officers and women staff to ensure that future employment patterns do not replicate, in slightly adjusted form, the same segregation between men's jobs and women's jobs as existed previously. At present, most women staff are very sceptical about future prospects for better jobs and better pay.

Discussion

The description of these two case studies concerned with defining and implementing 'equal opportunity' on opposite sides of the Atlantic has demonstrated the difficulty of creating and sustaining changes in the opportunity structures experienced by women and men in institutions of higher education. Broad differences and similarities of approach are identified in Table 5.1. Commitment to an action-research model in fact spans both North American and UK approaches, although it was more efficiently pursued in the USA as a result of a better-resourced, longer-term programme and the legislative requirement to monitor employment patterns. (Progress in computer-recorded personnel data in the UK is, however, making the profiling of employment patterns easier, cheaper and more accurate.) The main difference in emphasis on stages of the action-research model, however, resided in the identification of reasons for continuing inequalities and associated responses. In the USA the main, publicly-identified causes of inequality were described in terms of past informality and lack of standardisation in key personnel procedures, such as

Table 5.1 *Differences between US and UK approaches to implementing equal opportunities*

US	UK
1. Centralised administration	1. Decentralised/ collaborative
2. Authority via President of university	2. Uneasy relationship to university
3. Quantitative focus	3. Qualitative focus
4. Legislative power – based on contract compliance	4. 'Passive' legislation; compliance based on 'models of good practice', 'good will', campaign groups
5. Financed by university	5. Little access to university financing; progress by small short-term grants
6. Mixing of paid and unpaid labour	6. Functions mostly by unpaid labour

7. Commitment to action-research model:
   Collect data
   Verify by research
   Explore reasons
   Programmed response to address identified needs

recruitment, appraisal, promotion and selection for re-deployment or redundancy. The response was to emphasise the standardisation of personnel procedures and the standardisation of criteria for recruitment in terms of appropriate qualifications. In the UK case, the women involved were more interested in analysing inequality in terms of the structures of employment in the university and the routine exclusion of women from the better-paid, higher-status jobs. The response was partly to emphasis the need for more publicly accountable personnel procedures, but also to explore ways of challenging and breaking down, first, divisions between 'part-time', discontinuous and 'full-time, continuous working patterns, with their implications for access to training and development and, second, a grading structure for clerical and secretarial work which effectively tied women to a specific 'grade' by means of a formal job description and made it virtually impossible to move out of the 'secretarial' category into work recognised as administrative.

The North American university approach is thus closer to the formal EO model, which publicly emphasises standardisation of employment practice as the route to overcoming gender inequality. The UK project was not primarily committed to this model, but saw it as the only publicly legitimated route available.

Limits of the equal rights, access model of equal opportunities

The major problem with the model is the failure to engage with the nature of social relations in hierarchically-organised, elitist institutions of higher education. Women are seeking admittance to a male club, where the terms of entry are set by men-insiders. Major changes, which would reflect the interests and priorities of women, require major disruption of the club premises, rules and regulations and the wresting of control: nothing less then the right to re-define the goals of science, technology and management in terms other than the sole pursuit of weaponry and/or profit.

The liberal equal opportunities stance asserts that the rational–legal model of employment is gender-neutral and that, once introduced, it will assert its own socially progressive logic. The experience of practice would suggest that the process of change is not so simple. The stance adopted here is that the model provides a strategy but not a final solution. Far from being institutions with unitary, common goals, universities and polytechnics have a diverse range of interested groups, pursuing a variety of goals, using different strategies, which are related to their structural positions in the hierarchy and associated access to resources. The 'formalisation' of employment practices, along rational–legal lines, is interpreted differently by different groups. At one end of the scale, management, as in the US case study, may present it as a guarantee of fair practice and defence of the status quo, hence legitimising current inequalities. At the other end, women's groups and trade union officers may use it as the basis of a campaign for improved opportunities. The danger of this is that only those women who are willing or able to accept the current individualistic norms of higher education will have access to career jobs. The interest which many women express in working communally or collectively, and not necessarily pursuing a linear 'career' track, is regarded as inappropriate; raising children and managing the household is regarded as irrelevant experience and thus precluded for women in 'professional' jobs, and so on.

According to the EO model, racial and sexual discrimination are assumed to be unitary phenomena. In fact, they consist of a variety of processes. (The case studies of Jewson and Mason, 1986, and Jenkins, 1986, for example, show in some detail the complexities of discriminations made in the recruitment process.) In higher education, there are not only straightforward instances of exclusion of women, such as segregated recruitment to particular job categories and grades; but also numerous processes by which women's work is rendered secondary to men's work and women's abilities and interests are defined as inferior. Significantly, any intervention in the status quo is regarded as 'unfair' (and hence positively discriminatory in favour of women), because universities are supposed by definition to be gender-neutral.

The EO model is based on a notion of 'good practice' which has been espoused in personnel management texts for over 20 years, without showing great signs of social change. It is a model which advocates separating the analysis of the job from the analysis of the personal skills and technical abilities necessary to the job-holder. It is a technical model of recruitment which assumes that selection decisions can, and 'should', be made on the basis of technical qualifications, not social acceptability. There continues to be abundant evidence that recruiters are in fact very concerned about acceptability: whether applicants 'fit in'. They may have an articulated model of who 'fits in' and many quite openly say that they would not willingly appoint women because they are too disruptive of current working relations. (This is aside from other rationalisations about women's 'qualities'.) In fact, as Cockburn's (1983) analysis of the socially-constructed nature of 'technical skills demonstrates, it is practically impossible to make an absolute separation between 'technical' and 'social' criteria of selection and indeed between 'job' and 'job-holder', since the job is defined in relation to the person doing the work (see also Hollway, 1985).

The current financial situation has meant more short-term contracts, which disadvantage women by the loss of benefits such as maternity rights; little or no movement into profesional grades; 'informal' age limits on appointments (which discriminate against women who have been out of paid employment while raising children); cuts in courses in humanities and social sciences which have brought larger numbers of women into higher education; and emphasis on the single criterion of 'A' level grades for entry (which discriminates against mature-age women with domestic responsibilities who may want, and need, to gain qualifications in order to be able to find better-paid employment). The situation is thus not promising.

Undoubtedly, women's organisations, nationally and locally, will continue to rely on the equal opportunities approach, because of its legitimacy in terms of government and with employers and educators. The equal opportunities rhetoric, in other words, is useful in the fight for greater access to courses, jobs and incomes, whether or not the underlying philosophy is accepted at face value: it can at least be used opportunistically, given that there is some moral commitment behind it.

At a local level, the experience of the UK project leads the author to conclude that it is vital to set *very* limited targets for intervention (for example, *one* of the following: child care provision; health care for women staff; training for use of new office technologies; a survey on sexual harassment; and so on). This avoids the sense of being overwhelmed by the awfulness and generality of social disadvantages faced by women, while allowing a sense of progress on a limited front. It seems clear that women's groups and networks are vital to the success of local projects: not only are they a means of support, friendship and a source of security, but they ensure that the issues are identified and defined by women, who have the opportunity to explore what they would want to see as alternative employment practices. It also seems worth creating a routine, centralised monitoring procedure, carried out by the personnel department, and published annually: policy statements and re-appraisals of current practice can follow from this, but in the end, their success depends on changing the men's views of the service and support work carried out by women. They are unlikely to do this in the absence of collective action by women.

Nationally, it is necessary to campaign through trade unions, political parties and public bodies such as the Women's National Commission, the EOC and, in higher education, via the UGC and NAB, for more flexible (as opposed to rigidly standardised) approaches to employment, which nevertheless do not divest people of incomes sufficient to provide reasonable standards of living.

Lastly, women's groups need to keep on producing and talking over a critical analysis of current forms of higher education. In order to avoid entrapment in the status quo, it is important to have a vision of the alternatives: what would universities run with women holding half of the policy-making positions look like? Would 'degrees' still exist in a similar form? If so, who would be the judge of merit? What kind of planning and decision-making structures would we want? Would the science–arts division last, or would we change our definition of the conventional disciplines? Would we think in terms of post-18 education in a less linear, time-constrained fashion? How should we strike the balance between autonomy and account-ability (Scott, 1986) where 'academic freedom' is not invoked as an excuse to exclude women from influencing academic priorities, because they happen to have different interests and definitions of worthwhile research and academic enterprise?

6

Just inside the counting house: women in finance

LYNN ASHBURNER

Introduction

An understanding of the position of women employees in the finance sector is of significance not just for those women themselves but for the wider consideration of how changing patterns of work are affecting women. As an expanding and successful part of the economy, the finance sector has had to develop new and flexible systems to deal with the ever changing environment. It is, as a consequence, at the forefront in the development and use of new technology. Banks and building societies spend three times as much and insurance companies twice as much on new technology than any other industry, when expenditure is taken as a percentage of turnover (*Financial Times*, 19 December 1986). With new technology comes new work patterns, new types of work and the possibility of new opportunities for women.

In the 1940s and 1950s there was considerable resistance by the banks to women becoming cashiers. One of the arguments used as justification was the assumed lack of acceptance by both customers and clients to having their money or financial affairs dealt with by women. Just how much things have changed is now apparent with the overwhelming majority of cashiers throughout the sector being women. Arguments against women's inherent ability to do jobs at all levels are difficult to sustain. So a closer examination of the 'reasons' given for women's continued lack of success in reaching levels of middle and higher management is clearly needed. This chapter considers the major ways in which women's roles continue to be restricted within the finance sector.

It would be wrong to assume that the changes that have occurred since the 1940s have led to any fundamental change in the patterns of sexual divisions of labour within the finance sector, as elsewhere. What needs to be examined therefore is the *persistence* of the ideology which continues to restrict women to support and service roles. This ideology also finds expression in the structures of organisations and in their personnel policies, particularly their recruitment and promotion systems. Women's restriction to the domestic sphere has left the public sphere an area which is male dominated and it is within this sphere that power and influence presides. To understand the resilience of the sexual division of labour it is important to recognise it as a system of power relations between men and women. There are few commodities that are more symbolic of that power than money.

The finance sector employs around 800 000 people almost half of whom are women (Department of Employment, 1983). The industry covers a multiplicity of organisations including banks, building societies, insurance and finance companies. Eighty per cent of the sector's current employment is in the three main areas of banking (44 per cent), insurance (27 per cent) and building societies (8 per cent). The proportion of women in this sector is slightly higher than the national average of 44.5 per cent, but there are variations within the sector. The building society industry has the highest level of female employment (over 70 per cent). Despite their numerical strength the one factor which is common throughout the sector is the heavy concentration of women in the lowest grades. It is the 'nature' of the industry that it has a high proportion of predominantly routine clerical jobs.

It is important to recognise that the employment structures and the policies adopted by most financial organisations, combined with widely held assumptions by most male managers – that women are not serious about careers – result in women themselves 'recognising' their very limited opportunities and limiting their ambitions likewise. It is women's *experience* of work and lack of opportunities which frequently leads them to rationalise their ambitions or to channel them in other directions. The effect of this is the creation of a vicious circle in which these two processes combine to produce a situation whereby very few women achieve promotion beyond the lower levels of management. However unintentional this may be it has the same effect as a deliberate decision to restrict the career opportunities of women.

Patterns of employment

Banking

The number of staff in the main five clearing banks almost doubled between 1959 (105819) and 1974 (208965) with the proportion of women increasing from 40 per cent to 55.5 per cent over the same years. By 1982 over the whole banking industry 57 per cent of staff were female (Department of Employment, 1983). This pattern of growth reflects the increase in bank transactions and the broadening of banking services. Since 1971 business growth has accelerated, averaging an annual 8 per cent increase in productivity, whilst the employment rate has decelerated, with an average 3 per cent annual growth. The continuing development and use of micro-electronics, which began in the 1960s, is given by Rajan (1985) as the main reason for the relative decline in employment opportunities.

Every sphere of banking work is now technology-orientated and this has had an effect on the composition of banking staff. A *Financial Times* article (Groom, 15 April 1985) stated that, during 1984 alone there had been a fall of 300 in the number of full-time employees within the London clearing banks and an increase of 600 in the number of part-time workers. Bunyan and Youdale (1981) in their study of a major clearing bank suggest that the development of new technology has led to the restructuring of branch networks and as a consequence there has been a reduction in the number of managerial positions and an increase in routine clerical work.

The significance of these trends becomes clear when the position of women in the banking hierarchy is examined. Egan's 1979 study of the main clearing banks (1982) found that over 90 per cent of women were in clerical grades compared with 60 to 65 per cent of men. By contrast, over 90 per cent of employees in managerial and appointed categories, were male; fewer than 5 per cent of women fell into this category, compared with 35 to 45 per cent of men. Between 1974 and 1979 (which saw the implementation of EO legislation) the relative proportions of men and women in both clerical and managerial grades remained broadly the same.

Other studies substantiate these findings. Povall *et al* (1982) observe that the marked increase in the total numbers of women employed in this sector has not resulted in corresponding moves upwards into management. Those women who have been promoted do not, in the main have jobs related to mainline banking business and neither are they in jobs which are seen as essential experience for progress to top management. With new technology bringing reduced promotion prospects within branch work and the increase in routine non-career clerical work within banks, opportunities for women to progress are likely to be correspondingly fewer. The growth of special management trainee systems for graduates and high flyers may further reduce opportunities for the progress of other employees up through the ranks into management.

Insurance

Within the insurance sector total employment levels have risen only slightly, between 1960 and 1974 there was a 17 per cent increase in staff (DoE; 1983). From 1971 to 1976 the number of male employees declined by 10000 (7 per cent) not rising to the 1971 figure again until 1982. Over the same period (1971–82) female employment experienced a steady rise showing a total increase of 16 per cent. With the oil crisis in 1973 came two years when there was an annual decline of 8 per cent. This was followed by a modest recovery but over-capacity within the industry prompted rationalisation with reductions in staff and branch networks. Since 1977 the growth rate has only averaged 2 per cent per annum and so the process of rationalism has continued. Reductions in clerical staff have largely been offset by increasing numbers in computer related and life business sales areas. In Rajan's sample of 66 companies, the decrease in clerical jobs was projected to range between 5 and 30 per cent.

Areas of growth in employment have been primarily in areas of male employment, whereas the area of expected decline is predominantly female. As Ryan and Medlam's study (1984) of several large insurance companies shows, the increasing use of information technology means that the work of insurance branches can be conducted by relatively unskilled employees equipped with computers. The decline in the range of skills at branch level is resulting in a polarisation between these workers and the highly skilled specialists at head office. Their findings show that even in large offices where women can outnumber men, very few women are employed at a professional level, being mostly typists, telephonists and clerks. They believe that women's careers in the industry are currently at risk since women are less able to equip themselves with specialist qualifications and skills, because the bridge between lower and higher level roles via work experience may be disappearing due to the increasing use of computers.

Another study, by Collinson and Knights (1985), concludes that in life insurance, apart from a few specialist fuctions, the main route to a career in management is through sales, but that women are largely absent from this sphere of work. They note that women remain almost exclusively in subordinate clerical positions. These trends are affecting women's employment prospects within the insurance industry both quantitatively and qualitatively, resulting in the likelihood of fewer jobs and fewer opportunities for women to develop careers.

Building societies

By 1985 the building society movement employed over 65500 people in 167 societies. This represents a remarkable 173 per cent increase, an average of 7 per cent per annum, over 24000 total for 1969 when figures were first kept. Rajan (1985) estimates that business volume has increased by between 8 and 15 per cent per annum. The figures for growth in total assets are considerably higher. (For example, from 1978 to 1984 the top five societies had an annual average growth in assets of 18 per cent.) This growth rate has been facilitated by the expanding use of microelectronic technology.

There is considerable variation in size between the societies with 51 per cent of the industry's workforce employed by just the top five societies and over 90 per cent by the top 35 societies. Figures on the numbers of male and female employees have only been kept since 1979, when 65 per cent of all staff were female. By 1985 this had risen to over 71 per cent. This high level of feminisation has not led to a higher female involvement at management levels. My own research (Ashburner, 1986; and current work) has found that in both large and medium-sized societies women were employed primarily in the lower grades of management. Most societies have a two- or three-tier system of recruitment in which the stereotype of the female cashier and male manager is fairly rigidly adhered to. Women who have reached lower levels of management have invariably done so via internal promotion and at a much slower rate than their male colleagues. In those societies where men do perform the cashiering role, this is invariably seen as necessary experience prior to a move into management.

The continuing rapid development of technology within building societies, by aiding the development of new products, has increased branch work. However at the same time, higher productivity has led to a declining rate of staff increase in all parts of the organisations. Automation in the branches has resulted in fewer full-time cashiers and an increase in the number of part-timers with the work of both the full- and part-time staff having been deskilled. There is now less opportunity for clerical staff to acquire the experience necessary for promotion. With few new branches opening and a growing emphasis on professional qualifications, the reduction in opportunities will almost certainly have greater adverse effects on women's promotion.

Barriers to women's promotion

Recruitments

Both within banking and within building societies it has been common practice in the past to have a single level of recruitment with a certain minimum level of qualifications (usually four 'O' levels), whereby in theory at least all recruits, given sufficient ability and application, could progress up the career ladder. In practice of course, given the pyramidal employment structure this has never been the case. The requirement of such a system is that most recruits either leave or remain in the lower grades. Such a pattern fits easily with assumptions about women being poor career prospects and with the organisation's need for a large pool of relatively unskilled labour from which only a minority are selected to fill career posts.

The direct discrimination of the past which sustained this system has developed into more subtle forms of indirect discrimination.

More recently the trend has been towards the introduction of several levels of recruitment, for example, taking on more highly qualified staff as management trainees on accelerated training courses. Tiering recruitment is likely to reinforce the gender division of labour whereby those recruited on the traditional basis of four 'O' levels are not now able to progress beyond the routine clerical grades. In this way some existing career paths are being formally curtailed.

Thus a major factor in recruitment currently is differential selection on the basis of qualifications. In both banking and building societies the required educational qualification to commence the professional examinations is two 'A' levels or an equivalent. Egan (1982) quotes the 1979 figures for one major clearing bank where 31 per cent of male recruits had qualifications of two 'A' levels or above compared with only 11 per cent of women. Tarbuck's study (1984) of another of the big five banks shows that 27 per cent of male recruits had higher qualifications compared with only 8 per cent of women. In a study of one major building society (Ashburner, 1986) which operated a single recruitment system, it was found that in an interview sample of 37 branch staff only 3 of the 28 female employees had qualifications of two 'A' levels or an equivalent, as compared with all of the 9 male employees. As one female member of staff who had two 'A' levels said: 'I doubt that I'd have been two years on the counter if I'd been a man with my qualifications.' Several of the female cashiers had been studying for 'A' levels which they had decided to abandon in favour of taking a job with the society. None of them had been aware at recruitment of the need for 'A' levels in order to commence the professional exams.

Povall *et al* (1982) note that an analysis of applications and interviews with managers within British banks showed that the emphasis on higher qualified men and lower qualified women was not a result of chance. These forms of deliberate discrimination enable management to justify the promotion of men ahead of women on the basis of qualifications alone. Collinson and Knight's study of recruitment into life insurance sales also shows how the use of informal networks almost guaranteed that sales remained a male preserve. The preferred means of recruitment was to draw on an internal labour market of trainees. Only under severe business pressure and as a last resort would they advertise either through recruitment agencies or in the press.

What is required of their career staff by an organisation is explained at recruitment. This usually involves a long-term commitment, the advisability of becoming professionally qualified and in some circumstances the probability of having to move with the job. In describing these requirements, it is clear that they could be presented as a positive encouragement to those viewed by management as having career potential but as a positive discouragement to those who do not align themselves with the typically 'male' profile of a career.

Professional qualifications

In the insurance industry the Chartered Insurance Institute provides two levels of qualification, the Associateship (CACII) and the Fellowship (FCII), and there are three classes of members. Ordinary members must be employed in insurance and pay a membership subscription; approximately 17 per cent are women (Ryan and Mcdlam, 1984). It is not necessary to be a member in order to take the ACII or the FCII qualifying examinations. To qualify for the ACII candidates must pass a qualifying examination, be aged over 21 and have at least two years' experience in insurance. Approximately 6 per cent of professional members at this level are women. At the highest level, the FCII, approximately 3 per cent are women. Most companies are prepared to sponsor employees on these courses but it is usual for this facility to be withdrawn after the employee's mid-twenties. This disadvantages any woman returning to work after a family who wants a career in insurance.

In banking, career staff are encouraged to take banking qualifications but despite theoretical equality there are still very few qualified women. Egan suggests that although women are no longer discouraged, they are not encouraged either and certainly not to the same extent as the men. Povall *et al.* (1982) point out that banking staff have to be nominated in order to go forward to the examinations and for women this means dependency upon the sponsorship of a sympathetic manager. Even with day release, study takes up a lot of personal time for a period of several years, and women will tend not to see the potential reward for such effort when they know of very few women in senior banking positions.

Most staff are only eligible for study leave within the first few years after entry to the bank and this inevitably discourages women who are less likely to commit themselves to a career immediately upon entry, whether because of lack of encouragement or an under-assessment of their own ability and ambitions. As Egan shows, such problems are reflected in the data on Institute of Banking (IOB) qualification, where in 1980 women only formed 18.3 per cent of Ordinary IOB members, 3.4 per cent of Associates and 0.3 per cent of Fellows. In one major clearing bank out of almost 1700 branch managers only 7 were women, whilst in 2 other banks the numbers of women managers were only 5 and 4 (Egan, 1982).

The Chartered Building Societies Institute (CBSI) is the professional and examining body for building society staff. Professional qualifications have not played a major role in the development of career staff in the past but more societies are now beginning to encourage their staff to become qualified. Several factors have contributed towards this. The recent rapid expansion of branch managers are relatively young, and the previously fluid promotion systems now appear blocked. Unlike the banks, movement of personnel between societies is fairly common and often viewed as an alternative to internal promotion. This has deterred many from committing themselves to the required minimum of four years study. With increased competition for promotion, the holding of qualifications becomes an important measure of an individual's commitment to their careers. There is also a perceived need for building societies to present a more 'professional image' to the rest of the business world with the widening of their powers (1987 Act).

Figures from the CBSI show the total number of examination entries and completions for 1983–5. Whereas the number of completions averaged 320 per annum, the number of people studying for the examinations in any one year has risen to an average of 3800. The information on numbers of women entrants was unavailable but there was limited information on the numbers of women who had gained the Associates of the Chartered Building Societies Institute (ACBSI). This had risen from 3 in 1978 to 32 in 1984. This clear indication of the increased interest in qualifications suggests that it is increasingly the case that they may become essential for promotion beyond a certain level. Data from my current research (Ashburner, 1986) in this area shows that women are less likely than men to take professional qualifications. It was found that the great majority of younger full-time female staff said that they wanted a career but of the main factors which made them reluctant to invest too much time in training and qualifications was the fear that should they have children this would all be 'wasted', since the industry makes it very difficult for women to combine managerial work and having children: 'It's a bit frightening really when you think you might get there and then you might feel you want children and have to give it all up' (female cashier). In this society, of the 20 full-time female staff members interviewed, only 1 had children.

Without the requisite 'A' levels, a minimum of two years of study would be needed to gain an appropriate qualification for eligibility to the professional examinations. Add to this the minimum time of four years that it takes to become professionally qualified, plus the large amount of personal time that is involved, then the level of commitment demanded becomes clear. The six-year time limit for completing the examinations may be waived to allow for maternity leave but anyone who is not currently employed within a building society cannot begin the next stage. The fact that there were no women in senior management positions led many women here also to believe that is was simply not possible for a woman to be promoted beyond a certain grade. Even those women who were taking the professional examinations believed that their chances of promotion within their society were not as good as they were for men.

Policies on the recruitment of graduates varied considerably between companies. Specific graduate recruitment programmes are a fairly recent trend and there is little information available at present. One large building society introduced such a scheme in 1985 and of the 15 recruits 7 were women, which was considered by the society as visible evidence of their equal opportunity policy. In such cases this visibility factor could work to the advantage of women. The more common trend is for graduates to be taken on individually, where previously candidates with just 'A' levels were recruited. Ryan and Medlam 1984 found that the numbers were evenly split between men and women but they noted that when it came to considering women for promotion, *only* women who were graduates were considered.

Promotion patterns

Throughout the finance sector there is considerable job segregation by gender. In banking and insurance there are very few women employed in jobs which involve dealings with business and professional clients. In insurance there are very few women involved in life insurance sales. Managers again are making gender specific assumptions about a person's suitability for a certain type of work. Collinson and Knights show in their study that managers of insurance companies took it for granted that candidates would be male: 'The whole strength of our business is the capability of our man to project the company's image to our marketplace . . . To succeed that have to be recommended as a good class guy who knows what he's doing' (manager, quoted in Collinson and Knights, 1985, p 26).

There are two separate issues here. The first is that managers seldom question implicit assumptions that women cannot do certain types of work: 'It may sound sexist but I don't want women because it's not feasible for 22 year old girls to be sent up tower blocks of Hulme at 9 o'clock at night. We only have females for the jobs that females do better than males, which are typing, secretarial and part-time. Women don't make inspectors, they're not successful in the long term' (insurance manager quoted in Collinson and Knights, 1985, p. 27).

Their rationale usually includes a reference to the customer who it is believed would not be prepared to accept a woman in that role. Collinson and Knights quote another manager in insurance: 'A woman can't do business over a pub lunch. She can't say "come on let's go out for a pie and a pint" can she? Because the wrong connotation is placed on it' (p. 36).

When the job involves joining informal, social networks which are invariably male orientated, this need not pose problems for women. Ryan and Medlam found that in insurance, management attitudes were that women did not want selling jobs and that they did not have the personality necessary for sales. During my research, interviews with two women who had gained experience at such development work within building societies clearly showed that these problems had not affected their ability to perform their job satisfactorily. The reaction of clients occasionally may have been one of surprise but it was also one of acceptance. As one of these women development managers explained:

Telephone calls are easily forgotten so when you take them out to lunch they remember you. I have got to know the solicitors round here and going out to lunch poses no problems. An older solicitor once asked me if we could go to a pub further out of town just in case he was recognised, in case word got back to his wife!

Another woman makes plain some of the 'advantages' of being a woman in the job:

You make yourself known to a lot of people. You must make sure that people are aware of your products and I'm in a lot of organisations, the Chamber of Commerce, for instance, and different supper clubs where you meet professionals . . . You always get this kind of joke that women always get in because of curiosity. If curiosity gets me in the door then curiosity is great. There are a few disadvantages as a lot of contacts are amongst men who play golf or snooker together . . . I do go along and have a go . . . They know that I can do most things but you are still not treated the same. I will attempt to do things that blokes do but I don't push it. They would not take me seriously and I'm not into being male anyway. I win because I offer a good service, I do a lot more than perhaps a male counterpart would do.

The second issue raised is that such jobs are considered as essential experience for any subsequent promotion thus creating a 'Catch-22' situation. Collinson and Knights found that some insurance companies quite openly admitted that because trainee staff were usually promoted to sales work, they would only employ men. Even if such jobs continue to be predominantly male, there can be little justification for insisting on sales experience before considering a person for promotion to a job which does not involve outside sales work. No examples could be found of predominantly female jobs which were considered to be essential experience before promotion could be offered. All-female jobs such as typing had very low ceilings in terms of career paths and it could be difficult for typists to transfer to non-typing grades in order to progress further. The anomaly is emphasised by instances found of building society branch managers who had been recruited directly into their jobs without any previous building society experience, who admitted that they left the running of the branch 'to the girls' because they were not familiar with all the routine work.

As Egan observed, promotion procedures rely heavily on subjective assessments rather than on objective criteria and may be subject to preconceived expectation about women as career prospects (Egan, 1982). Within banking it is still a common practice to fill vacancies by appointment. Whereas this also happens in some building societies, it is more usual for the majority of vacancies to be advertised.

Where an annual staff appraisal scheme exists it should offer an opportunity for all staff to let their managers know what their job expectations are. Ideally the manager should let the employee know what the criteria are for promotion and also allow them to see the asessment for themselves. In practice these schemes are heavily dependent upon the subjective assessments of (primarily) male managers who have probably not been trained to be sensitive to the issues and aspirations of female staff. When a third party from the personnel department is involved, as was the case in one major building society, then the women employees were more satisfied that their ambitions were being taken seriously. Most banks have appraisal schemes but only a few of the larger building societies do. Whatever their weaknesses they are preferable to the situation that exists in many medium-sized societies where female staff are simply never considered for promotion into management.

Where management development programmes exist or accelerated training programmes are available for a few individuals, the decision about placement is usually made at recruitment. There is the problem therefore that they may merely reflect prevailing expectations or prejudices about women's prospects. In two clearing banks the system is so formalised that staff are put onto a series of tiers. The system then becomes self-fulfilling since those on the lower tiers are given less training. Where such programmes are designed around individuals, those members of staff not on such programmes experience reduced promotion prospects and can find it difficult to gain entry to the programme at a later time.

Except at junior levels and for some specialist roles, the emphasis in these industries is on internal promotion. The main 'organisational' block to women's promotion in the insurance industry was identified as 'management attitudes towards women'. Management attitudes are a primary factor underlying all the structural blocks which have so far been discussed.

Management attitudes

The most common generally-expressed management view throughout the sector was that the present employment pattern was satisfactory and that equal opportunities did exist. It was a question of whether women were prepared to take those opportunities, to show commitment and to achieve a satisfactory work performance. Typical of management attitudes were:

> I can't see why females can't get to the top, I think it is just lack of motivation on the part of the females. (Building society branch manager)

> With equal opportunities we have been involved in establishing . . . a full picture of our work force. All the new recruitment procedures that have been introduced have been with those in mind . . . You are employed, you are doing a good job, but if you do want to go further then you as an individual have got to meet these requirements [mobility and professional qualifications etc.] We do not consider them discriminatory in any way . . . The resignations tend to peak for females at seven, eight and nine years . . . We have not got any information on the numbers of women in higher management . . . to be seen to be fair we always put the right person into the job, we don't care if they are male or female, it is almost discriminatory to try to look at this and distinguish. (Personnel manager of a major building society)

Ryan and Medlam found that management in insurance companies were more likely to see the blocks to women's career progress as residing in women's own limitations. Yet as their research revealed, it is executives' attitudes and company policies which are most likely to disadvantage women in the organisation.
Managers assume that women are only interested in lower clerical

jobs and are not as ambitious as their male colleagues because this is how they observe their own staff structure. This is used to justify the existing systems and attitudes. What is not being taken into account is the extent to which women's experiences of the inequalities of employment have led them to feel a sense of resignation, realism or rationalisation about their situation. An awareness of the obstacles that they face both at work and at home, which do not affect the majority of men, can be a very powerful deterrent. Just as all men are not equally ambitious neither are all women but if women's opportunities are severely limited then they are denied the freedom of choice.

There is also a danger that if the 'problem' of unequal opportunities and the sexual division of labour is only seen in terms of increasing the opportunities for women to be employed on the same terms as men, then this is acceding to the predominant value system which sees men's employment as more 'important' than women's. This devaluing of the female role can be seen in the way that any job which becomes accepted as 'women's work' is invariably low paid and almost never done by men.

Many managers perceived women as being more committed to the domestic sphere than to having a career with the assumption that a wife's job is always secondary to a husband's. As one building society branch manager explained:

> A woman taking a job, the structure of the society is such that it is less likely that it will be a career position. It is often an extra income and the husband's job would be the career position. For a woman to take an assistant manager's position would involve moving branch, which could well involve moving house which could involve the husband having to change his job. So unless she has the career position and the husband is a typist somewhere, he would say that he couldn't move.

Thus the prospect that most women employees would at some stage have a family and go on maternity leave or opt for childcare may be used by employers as a rationalisation for attitudes and policies which work against the achievement of equal opportunities. The extent to which such beliefs shape attitudes and gave an adverse effect on women's careers, can result in the operation of a self-fulfilling prophecy.

Part-time work

Given that the statutory level of maternity leave is inadequate for many women and child care facilities are very poor, most women take advantage of part-time work at the high price of inferior terms and conditions of work with a loss of career prospects. Supervisory and management positions are not available on a part-time or shared basis. Therefore transferring to part-time work invariably means moving to the lowest grade, to more routine, less interesting work and often also to a lower rate of pay. Yet growth in the level of part-time work has occured in most parts of the finance sector and this is a trend that is going counter to the development of careers for women.

Within the London clearing banks there was an increase in 1984 of 60 part-time employees. Within the building society industry the percentage of part-time staff has grown from just 4 per cent in 1971 to over 19 per cent in 1985. In many medium-sized societies at least 50 per cent of cashiers are now part-time. The percentage of part-time workers in the insurance industry has remained fairly steady at around 11 to 12 per cent.

The trend towards the use of part-time workers has been facilitated by the development of new technologies within many offices, which have had the effect of diskilling jobs. Evidence from the building society sector shows that whereas prior to the introduction of front office terminals, cashier training took two to three weeks, it now only takes two to three days (Ashburner, 1986). Jobs such as cashiering and clerical work are regarded as primarily female jobs and this has made it possible for them to be opened up as areas of part-time employment. Such development offers several advantages to the employer – lower salary costs, more flexibility and hence reduced staffing levels and lower training costs. By increasing the percentage of part-time workers, organisations are also indirectly reducing pressure on promotion systems which due to lack of employment growth are seen to be blocked.

In fact by recruiting only married women with children who have previous experience within the finance area, the need for training is reduced. There is also a large number of women who wish to return to work after having a family. That married women with children end up in low-paid part-time work appears to be more a result of their vulnerability than of their conscious preference. Part-time workers are denied access to any jobs other than the lowest paid; this results in employment practices which most women find it difficult to escape from. Such practices, by discriminating against married women with children who wish to remain in employment, create the pool of cheap labour that employers willingly exploit.

Positive action initiatives

Most companies within the finance sector do not operate positive action programmes or send their female employees on women-only training courses. It is important that the initiatives which are described here are seen in this context. The type of action being taken varies considerably between companies but however limited most of these actions are it is important to recognise them as vital first steps. New initiatives need to be developed further and precedents need to be set that other companies might follow. What needs to be considered is the scope of any programme, who is eligible for it and what the impetus for its introduction was.

Within three major banks the development of retainer schemes and positive action training has been the result of either pressure from the trade unions, the presence of an individual (usually a woman) within the management structure who was prepared to push for such developments or threat of a formal investigation by the EOC. The shortcomings of these schemes is their present very limited application.

The National Westminster Bank was the first, in January 1981, to set up a re-entry scheme whereby women and men could take a break in their career for a maximum of five years to care for young children. Under this scheme the bank guaranteed to offer re-employment to an individual at the same level of appointment or grade at which they left. They would also provide a training programme on their return designed to update their knowledge and competence. However, the scheme is only open to 'those who are seen to have the potential to reach senior management and who expect to return to work with their career commitment undiminished'. They also run what they call a reservist scheme under which there is no commitment by the bank to re-employ an individual but the bank will consider participants for suitable vacancies at the level of employment or grade at which they left the bank. This scheme is open to 'those who are seen to have the potential to reach junior/middle management and who expect to return to full time employment'.

Applicants for these schemes are expected to have completed at least 5 years' service and on their return have a minimum of 26 years years to serve before retirement. Participants must give an undertaking to provide a minimum of two weeks' paid relief work per year and attend an annual one-day seminar. They are also encouraged to continue their studies for the Institute of Bankers examinations. At March 1986 there were 14 staff on the re-entry scheme and 54 on the reservist scheme, from a total of over 20000 female employees. The intention at the outset was to keep the criteria for selection high and the number of women involved were expected to be low (Adams, 1981). The scheme was introduced because the bank recognised the difficulties being faced by women who wanted a carer and a family and could not fulfill the 15 to 20 years of unbroken service that were required to reach branch management. It is very much in the banks' interest to introduce such a scheme. Women are working long before starting families, have greater awareness of their own capabilities and thus are working their way further up the career ladder before they leave. Thus the value of the experience and training that they represent to the bank is considerable.

More recently the bank has introduced a managment development course for women and has integrated equal opportunities awareness training into its main management training programme. The course for women includes two separate weeks of full-time study, an intervening company-based project under tutorial guidance and a one-day follow-up workshop. The course, like the re-entry scheme, is designed for 'women of real potential' and aims to provide guidance in management skills and to develop confidence. If women are to be encouraged to reach higher management it is in the bank's interests again to ensure that they are well trained. These schemes undoubtedly benefit those women who are on them but do little for the majority of women who work in banks. A true commitment to equal opportunities by the banks would involve the removal of barriers to women's progress at all levels within the organisation.

In August 1985 the Midland Bank introduced a similar retainer scheme. Like the Nat West, they too specify that staff may take only

one period of absence for a maximum of five years which, in the case
of women, runs from the end of their maternity leave. At January
1986 there were 10 women participating on the scheme out of a total
again, of over 20000 female emloyees. Prior to the introduction of
the scheme a series of two-day workshops were run for all senior
personnel to raise their awareness of sex equality issues. There were
also several week-long developmental courses run for women
managers. It was felt to be essential to 'prepare the ground' in this
way to ensure that the scheme would be accepted and would work
effectively. As the Group Equal Opportunities Manager explained,
new systems on their own may not be enough, there is a need to
change attitudes before systems can really change. Any attempts to
raise the consciousness of male managers can only be welcomed.
However, given the entrenched attitudes and existing recruitment
and promotion practices the value of a two-day workshop without
considerable and sustained follow-up, could well be limited in terms
of changing attitudes, let alone systems.

The Group Equal Opportunities Unit was set up at Midland Bank
in 1984 with responsibilities for ethnic minorities and disabled
people as well as for women. The unit has promoted changes in
appraisal procedures and training so that women staff are
encouraged to develop their careers to the same extent as men.
Besides the organising and running of courses, it also monitors
statistics on recruitment, promotion and training. It makes such
information available to the trade unions at regular joint meetings.

In 1986 Barclays introduced their career break scheme. Although
only 3.5 per cent of their managers, in December 1985, were women
this this was slightly better than the other main banks where figures
range from 2 per cent to 1.5 per cent. One of the main differences of
this scheme is that participants have a choice between taking a
two-year break or continuing to work for two years on a part-time
basis whilst remaining at their present grades. Barclays is therefore
the only bank that allows for management work to be done on a
part-time basis. Their scheme is open to anyone who has at least 5
years' service and has reached clerical grade 4 and above, if they
have also got either the Institute of Bankers exams or an equivalent,
or are on clerical grade 8. After the 2 year period the participant
must resume full-time working and will be re-employed on the same
salary plus any general increments. Within 6 months of the scheme
commencing there were a total of 35 women on it, 20 were working

part-time, 7 had opted for the break in service and eight were still on maternity leave.

The trade unions have played an *extremely* important role in raising awareness of all the issues surrounding equal opportunities and BIFU (Banking, Insurance and Finance Union) have set up their own EO committees in several banks. They welcome the new developments and the retainer schemes but with reservations. If equal opportunities are to become a reality for the huge majority of women in the finance sector then such schemes need to be extended and expanded.

BIFU has also been involved with the development of positive action training courses within several finance companies. The first course was for women only to enable them to assess their career situations and the follow-up course was for line management, with the objective of increasing their awareness of the need for positive action. Funding from the MSC has enabled individual and group counselling to continue once a month for a year. It is also seen as necessary to run courses which include women members of staff and line management so that differing attitudes can be more closely examined and discussed. An important objective was that women from all levels of the organisation should be included so that the courses would not be seen as elitist.

The impetus for change can also arise from within organisations themselves. The Women and Work Programme has developed a training programme for women in the Prudential Insurance Company. The Manpower Services Commission and the Industrial Society with their 'Women in Insurance' project have also helped to raise the level of debate within the insurance industry and to identify an EO programme which will 'meet the particular needs of individual companies'.

The building society sector lags a considerable way behind even the tentative developments that are taking place in banking and insurance. The three largest societies have sent individual women on women-only training courses and two of these societies are running Women into Management courses. There was adverse publicity generated when the Leeds Building Society was investigated by the Equal Opportunities Commission between 1979 and 1982, and was found to have committed unlawful acts of direct and indirect discrimination against women. This may have encouraged other large societies to examine their recruitment and promotion procedures but there is no indication that the majority of medium-sized and small societies have taken any action in this area.

What is needed is an increased awareness on the part of both staff and management of the issues surrounding equal opportunities. This is where the role of a union or a staff association can be crucial. The absence of unions from large parts of the finance sector, most notably building societies, corresponds with areas of few initiatives. Within banking and the insurance industry the unions have been very important in pushing for positive action. Given their low level of representation in building societies and the predominance of what are seen as more pressing problems such as the effects of mergers, the unions here have yet to address positive action issues, It is also evident that strong support from at least part of the management hierarchy can be of great importance.

The problem with many of the current developments towards equal opportunities is that the concept of work and career is still seen very much in male terms. The emphasis is on developing and changing the women so that they are able to fit in with existing organisational structures. If programmes are solely concerned with the personal development of women they could be seen to be dealing with only half the problem. This again depends how the problem itself is defined in the first place. Margaret Stone (1984) writing in the *Building Society Gazette* gives an example:

> the Abbey National building society called in the Industrial Society to discover if major obstacles were impeding the progress of women in the society. The Industrial Society concluded that there were none; it was just that women failed to make use of available opportunities. (p. 7)

This perception misses the need for progress towards changing the structures themselves so that they can respond to women's specific requirements or to changing the concept of what the qualities are that managers need. What changes there have been, such as the career break schemes, have come about primarily in response to the needs of the organisation rather than to the needs of women workers. There has been no progress, for example, towards improving the terms of employment of part-time workers, a move which would bring immediate benefit to a large number of women.

The initiatives which have been described are just a *very* small beginning. The role of pressure from within and without has been particularly important in this sector and may well continue to be in the future. That is whilst managerial attitudes remain generally convinced that the status quo is the most desirable. The push for change, for new directions, has not come from management but 'prime movers', mainly from women and trade unions who will need encouragement and support if they are not to be either wasted or exhausted. The growth of support networks and organisations such as Women in Banking is therefore to be welcomed and vital. But this 'boom' sector of the UK economy so far shows the negative as well as the positive possibilities for women's increased numeric presence in the work force. Here women are being under-valued and pressured into an acceptance of the status-quo, for a place 'just inside the counting house'! The few positive developments that have taken place need all the help they can get if they are to be more than exceptions to this general current situation.

7

Who's changing whom?
Women, management and
work organisation

JANE SKINNER

Introduction

Women remain at the margins of the powerful positions in the world
of work, despite a range of formal and informal policy guidelines
'designed' to stop discriminatory practices and change traditional
attitudes. Contributors to this book have given their own views on
the range of reasons for changes in women's status at work being
slow and outcomes, so far, very mixed. Positive specific actions to
accelerate change remain vital and much needed, as most of the
chapters have stressed.

If such action is to foster change beyond the individual level then
it must include changes in organisation culture, work processes and
roles at work. Various views of *how* such changes can be fostered
through analysis, training, policy development and 'experiment'
have been set out earlier. This chapter seeks to build on these
discussions by considering the implications of individual women's
progress at work for changes in the practices of, indeed the
definitions of 'policy' and 'management', within work
organisations.

Different rationales for positive action – and different prime targets

As with rationales for promoting equality of opportunity, those making a case for taking positive action draw on 'alternative' beliefs and ideologies about rights, roles and socio-economic systems. Whilst labelling these may be simplistic, it may help avoid the grosser general assumption that those in favour of positive action share the same beliefs and have identical goals. There *are* discernible groupings of rationales for supporting positive action concerning women at work. Table 7.1 below sets out the possible range of stances underpinning positive action approaches.

Table 7.1 *Why take positive action? Possible rationales*

Theme	Access 'opening'	Individual career progress	Changing ways of working	Changing patterns and structures
Aims/ goals of positive action	Overcoming barriers to individual opportunity	Opening up individual opportunities to get in/ get on work	'Equalising' and changing work at processes and rewards (nb management)	Restructuring organisational 'forms'
Main strategy	Remove formal blocks; 'open' doors to choices	Encourage 'pioneer' career/job approaches	Changes in decision-making approaches	Revise hierarchic structure and control approaches
Typical activities	1 Training individual women 2 Legislation to remove formal blocks	1 Training groups of women 2 Attitude training for men and women working together 3 Personnel practice changes to help women at work	1 OD/process experiments 2 Women taking charge regularly 3 Policy changes 4 Reward and status changes	1 Experiment with new collaborative decision making and work management 2 New work-day/ working year/ working life patterns 3 Different processes and roles in managing work

Table 7.1   *cont:*

Theme	Access 'opening'	Individual career progress	Changing ways of working	Changing patterns and structures
Underlying assumptions	*'Meritocratic' view'*	*'Radical social justice view'*	*'Structural cultural view'*	*'New paradigm view'*
	Individual injustices can be overcome by establishing rights. Little organisation change required	Individual injustice can be overcome by adjustments within the organisation and some special measures	Male dominance expressed in established ways of organisation working – women's progress is changing these	Female contribution at work valued if structures and processes reflect women's (as well as men's) strengths and ways of working

It is important to understand that there *are various rationales* for taking positive action – just as the reasons for doing nothing range from considering intervention 'wrong' or 'misguided' to mere oversight. We need to understand what 'positive action' can mean before we can discuss its effects and effectiveness. A range of rationales is set out in Table 7.2.

Table 7.2   *Positive action: strategies and rationales*

Main strategy	Training of women for higher status	Training of women and men Re attitudes and practices (NB managers)	Development of personnel practices and policies	Organisation developmentment experiments in work processes and roles	Changes in structures and management approaches/ roles
Prime 'change' focus of strategy	INDIVIDUAL CHANGE	←————————	————————→		ORGANISATIONAL CHANGE

Focus – individual change

Some supporters of positive action see it as being entirely about accelerating individual change so that women will become more 'evenly distributed' in the existing authority structures and culture of work organisations. Associated with this view can be beliefs about women's having to 'catch up' with men from a state of *deficiency* or a *'handicapped'* position, in the competition for 'male' jobs, particularly those of higher status. Alternatively those supporting change in individual rights and opportunities may believe women should expect specific positive action to *compensate* for past inequality or injustice.

The motivation for wishing to promote individual and indeed, statistical changes in where women are in work structures may be predominantly social, moral or economic. The force of moral arguments based on views of social justice can be key factors in triggering a 'push' for change. Women and men as citizens, workers, clients/consumers and often parents have views, not necessarily wholly dictated by socialisation and situation, concerning what constitutes the 'right order' in the world of work. This can impel individuals and small groups to push, against the odds, for taking direct positive action often beginning informally and even covertly. The role of such 'prime movers' or 'pioneers'[1] who believe in combating injustice or 'ineffectiveness' by positive action is vitally important in moving women's unequal status at work on to the agenda in organisations – whether these be companies or public authorities. To achieve this is a major success in many organisation cultures; especially so, since women's position at the bottom is still regarded by many as both normal and what many women want.

However, the trigger for taking positive action may be primarily economic. (Conversely, the biggest single barrier to removing discrimination at work is the economic one; the beliefs and realities about the pay and conditions women will accept at work.) Recognising the need for positive, specific activity to gain and retain skilled females as scarce talent in sections of our economy is growing. A leader article in *The Economist*, entitled 'Why Women Get the Jobs' (23 August 1986), pointed out that companies in growth sectors of European economies are increasingly hiring and promoting women to technical and management posts.

Certainly, changing individual perceptions, opportunities, position and rewards lies at the heart of taking positive action. Chapter 8 sets out ways in which fostering individual change in confidence, competence and position can be tackled. However we also have to consider positive action which see its prime focus as being changes in organisational process, roles and structures.

Focus – organisational change

Views of taking positive action which emphasise fostering organisational or structural change see the 'individual' focus as *either too narrow* or *as misguided*. Theories of 'deficiency' based on male and female difference or female 'handicaps' at work are seen as, at worst, 'blaming' the victim of discrimination at work. At the least, such views tend to leave the prime responsibility for effecting change in womens' role at work with individual women. Women may well be the only ones wishing for change but conventional management development theory sees change being best initiated at the top. So a focus on positive action to foster *organisational* change in working processes, roles and even structures seeks to address the reinforcing 'power' barriers against women's progress at work, as well as building women's competencies and aspirations. *If taking positive action is to bring change beyond the individual level then its strategies must, arguably, focus directly on the formal policies and 'culture' of the work organisation.* Of course those supporting the 'individual' focus may argue that any reliance upon, or hope for, 'enlightened' management is foolish optimism; thus realism dictates a two-stage approach – first getting individual women into power positions and only then aiming for structural changes.

The structural view, however, sees positive action strategies in terms of 'not only but also . . . at any one time. Positive action is seen as *at once* aiming to foster 'movement' for women to combat their under-representation, particularly in higher status, technical and craft jobs *and*, at the same time, to accelerate changes in organisation's values which, if unchanged, will perpetuate the undervaluing and subordinating of female contributions and status at work. This inclusive view of positive action may see the long term achievement being that of 'balanced', 'non-macho' organisations which value differences in their work-force as well as numerically fair involvement of women throughout the work-force.

Positive action and managing work

Having set out the range of views concerning the definitions of positive action and prime aims for it, we now turn to its relationship to general trends in the management of work. Our experience in the Women and Work Programme with public and private sector employers is now considerable. Currently, 'progressive' employers perceive that, historically, women's potential contribution at work was not recognised and even that 'there was discrimination'. Most believe themselves to be fair meritocrats promoting talent irrespective of gender or race. Some may add, usually as a lighthearted afterthought, that possibly women still do have to prove their worth a little more strongly than their male counterparts before gaining higher positions. Many add, as an apologetic but firm footnote, that women are commonly their own worst enemies as they do not *apply* for 'higher' posts as well as, unfortunately, taking career breaks which results in their skills becoming out-dated.

There are also employers who positively value feminine qualities such as being effective in handling people sensitively, being persuasive and working with others in a collaborative and supportive way. Of these a few recognise that valuing must move from individual appreciation to developing practices which attract, reward and retain such people with such qualities.

Equally, a number of employers, particularly in the public sector, have responded to the legal and sometimes political pressures expressed in some legislation and more specifically by party political manifestoes. Policies have been instituted to stop discrimination against women at work and to bring about real equality of opportunity for females in some public authority's employ. A few local authorities have been particularly active in this way. Some instances of such activity are set out in Chapter 1 and Chapter 2.

The results of this response are, thus far, very mixed in terms of significant shifts in statistics. For example, the number of women who are in jobs carrying the formal imprimatur – the 'appelation controlée' – of 'Manager' remains limited and not significantly different from what it was 10, 20 or, by some measures, 50 years ago. Henning and Jardin's study (1978) as well as Hakim's work (1979), shows that, whilst the number of women managers have increased over time, so have the overall number of managerial posts. The proportion of management posts occupied by women has remained remarkably constant over the past sixty years at 18 to 20 per cent of all such posts. Also fairly constant is the percentage of top level posts – at 2 per cent. Other studies, for example Hunt (1975), showed that 50 per cent of all the work establishments surveyed employed no women at all in managerial or supervisory posts. In addition, more recent and so far unpublished research conducted within the Women and Work Programme indicates that the traditional 'homestead' areas of female management such as teaching, nursing, social work and personnel management, now appear to have both declining overall percentages of women in management, this being particularly marked at the top of organisations. Whilst appearances may be changing, sustained by a few individual and often famous role models, appearances may be deceptive and the underlying reality remarkably unchanging or even worsening.

What appears to be happening is an increase in numbers and proportions of women attaining managerial and technical posts in private sector organisations – particularly those in growth sectors – but optimism about this as the beginning of substantial change may be premature. The current growth is from there being almost no women in such posts to there being enough to register in statistics – but still as a small minority. The general statistics about women in managerial posts remain almost unchanged due to the decline of women occupying such posts in the 'homestead' areas for female managers, many of these being in the public sector.

However, there is little doubt that working patterns *are* changing. Continuous careers of full-time secure employment with steady upward progression as a prospect are fading as the 'norm' for employee success. A survey in 1984 by Zehnder International and the London Business School (1984) showed that many employers foresaw the typical manager of the future having a career with several employers, with breaks between careers. It also forecasted more multiple careers, with people undertaking a range of different and independent (for example freelance) jobs. Is this good news for women, many of whom are used to flexible, discontinuous career paths? If lengthy specialist track records are less significant, is this good news for women aspiring to management and other non-traditional jobs?

Few employers or managers seem to be making linkages between changes in working patterns and how work will be managed *or* to link this to possible changes in women's roles at work. Yet, arguably, unless such linkages are teased out and positively built on the advancement of women out of the female work ghettoes is likely to rest on the weak twin foundations of direct, short-term organisational self interest (survival) and/or of social justice (altruism).

Whilst 'musts' and 'oughts' are triggers for starting positive action they risk being experienced by their 'donors' and their 'recipients' as gifts or acts of obligation. A third possible reason exists if explicit links *are* made between changes in how work will be managed, organised and equalising opportunities for working women. Positive action would then be triggered by an exploratory motivation – with the goal of finding more effective ways of working and managing being the primary one. There is, of course, no imperative that will make this happen, save perhaps the growing recognition – even in the UK – that existing processes and approaches to getting work done are 'old fashioned' and competitive, survival reasons require a deliberate fostering of change.

How much longer can the 'forty-forty-forty' pattern (that is, a forty-hour week, forty weeks a year, over a forty year working life span) be regarded as the norm for paid employment? For women, particularly those who actually bear children, it never has been the norm. Women's 'failure' or potential 'failure' to fit this pattern undoubtedly, has been a major reason for their remaining 'ghetto-ised' in low-paid, low-status work. The Pepperell Unit's survey of Managers and Women in the Insurance Industry (Bargh *et al*, 1986) showed the way this works out in practice – as a vicious circle. A commentary on the survey stated 'womens career potential is not developed because it is assumed they will leave to have babies and yet, if they do return after childbirth, they are condemned for abandoning their children' (Meade-King, 1986). Yet maintaining or increasing the supply of 'forty-forty-forty' jobs is widely agreed to be beyond what is possible – even in 'advanced' economies.[2].

If large-scale unemployment is not to be permanent then a change in the pattern of work, indeed in how work is defined, seems inevitable and desirable. Such a change is particularly required by women – and other 'minorities' – who are currently marginalised and segregated in 'the labour market'. For many women the conventional definitions of what is and is not formal 'work' have long been at least partial if not patriarchal. For 'the working woman', as Martin and Roberts' (1984) large-scale survey showed, labour does not end at the close of paid work but is interspersed with carrying our most of housework and home management. If working patterns *are* to change – to less years of employed work, less hours per week of such work and more periods of 'vacation' – then this could be beneficial for women's prospects as workers. For in a society where career 'breaks' (that is, gaps in employment or paid work), part-time work and a variety of work-like experiences are 'normal', then women become less 'atypical' and hence less handicapped as serious employees. Indeed, they should, in view of their typical life patterns, become advantaged!

Of course, this assumes a degree of rationality in recruitment and personnel approaches which may not work out smoothly in practice. The long-established myth about women not wanting career progression is a comfortable one which, while believed, enables women to be excluded from promotion paths without the excluders feeling any guilt. Also new myths may well be in the making to prevent the logic of new employment patterns changing who is where in work organisations. But the possibility *does* exist that the changing patterns of employment and of how work is organised may extend rather than continue to restrict women's paid work opportunities and rewards. A work force characterised by more restricted hours and years of work wth less 'secure' employment, more self-employment and more home-based work is coming. This can also be a society which rediscovers life patterns where paid working hours cease to dominate adult existence and where many current rationales for marginalising women (and other 'minorities') may crumble. Of course, the possibility of maintaining 'total' unemployment for the 20 per cent and employment for the 80 per cent remains a strong one! Far-sighted employers can, therefore, see taking positive action as a way of accelerating their getting into gear for the working patterns of the future. The work of Charles Handy (1984) in particular explores some dimensions of the likely changes which can be fostered now to attain more effective *and* more equitable working patterns in the future.

In his work Handy also points up ways in which work organisations may change to accomodate and organise these new patterns of work made all the more feasible by the information technology 'revolution'. He writes of the contractual organisation, of paying fees for services to groups, of federal organisations and of 'professional' organisations characterised by 'flat' structures (Handy, 1984). Yet the ideologies and conventional wisdoms of management literature still largely express or assume views of organisational structures where 'leader' and 'led', manager and managed, are linked in clear hierarchies of role, activity and accountability.

The rational cycle of management activities – planning, decision-making, implementing and evaluating – may be recognised as occuring principally by working 'through other people', but the strong implication remains that these people are different and lesser in their contribution to these key processes than 'managers'. Of course, much management literature – and possibly many managers before the theory caught up – recognises that 'involving and engaging' styles of managing may be more effective in many situations than autocratic approaches. From McGregor (1960) to Mouton and Blake (1978) as well as the work of Hertzberg (1968) and that of Child (1981), writers have recognised the importance of common norms amongst workforce and management in underpinning excellence of performance and thus effectiveness in organisations. Popular management texts, such as *In Search of Excellence* (Peters and Waterman, 1982) and *The Change Masters* (Moss Kanter, 1984), have also stressed the import- ance of shared commitment amongst the whole workforce to organisational excellence and success. For example, Kanter says in the introduction to her most interesting book: 'Organisations that are change-oriented, then, will have a large number of integrative mechanisms encouraging fluidity of boundaries, the free flow of ideas and the empowerment of people to act on new information' (Moss Kanter, p. 32).

This recent literature, particularly, has questioned much of the 'rationalist' teaching about how effective management emerges. Based as most of the authors are in the USA, it is perhaps not surprising that this questioning has stopped short of re-examining the conventional hierarchies and processes which constitute the 'Corporation'. After all some American companies may be ailing but Peters and Waterman (1982) had no problem in finding large numbers of 'excellent' companies – who are internationally successful. Thus what this new literature sets out are 'simple' and people-focused approaches to evolving and sustaining performance-based, change-oriented corporations. Many of these 'new' approaches certainly reverse the trend – to 'complexify' and perhaps mystify the basic processes of management which was very strong in management writing and in the business schools in the 1970s and early 1980s. This unearths, perhaps, a key reason for the welcome accorded to, Peters and Waterman's work in particular! These authors talk of the essentials of effective management as 'motherhoods', but continue to see the managing being carried out – by managers. Thus new management messages are about managing effective change rather than changing management. This can be seen in the introduction to *In Search of Excellence*: 'We hope that what follows, then, will illuminate just what values ought to be shaped and managed and that we will thereby have helped to solve the leadership dilemma after all' (1982, p. 26).

But it *is* possible to imagine changes in how 'management' is viewed and defined. Such changes in definition may help innovative organisation development to be conceived – which will literally recognise and build on female contributions to work management. Such changes hold considerable potential, particularly in the UK where existing management models and processes are *not* particularly effective by either economic or social indicators. Current approaches exclude significant talents, particularly if held by women or black people whether females or male. Additionally, existing models of how work is managed may be obsolete. So, removing blocks to effectiveness may well mean that 'equalising work opportunities' and 'changing management' should best occur in tandem. Existing management approaches appear to be based on hierarchies, quasi-military and patriarchal approaches to organising work which may no longer be functional nor any more rational than a number of alternative ways of getting work done. Change beyond the cosmetic levels, of the humane 'loose-tight' organisation whose fundamental structure remains purely hierarchic, is feasible; it may well make for effectiveness as well as lessening women's exclusion from the male world of 'decision-making' and 'power'.

Viewing 'Management' almost wholly as a separate role set – and thus as being carried out more or less entirely by managers – can be seen as a masculine and old-fashioned perpective on organising work effectively and efficiently. It confuses task with position. It may be that viewing work management in this old paradigm way not only denies much de facto management work which is carried out by those in non-management roles but also obscures the positive potentials of organising work in different ways. If this is accepted, then changing women's role in the world of paid work, particularly in relation to management, becomes a wider issue directly linked to developing new models of management and new forms of organisation. For the focus of developing management moves away from 'getting the right people for key roles' to getting the right processes and rewarding the effective people. In this definition of changing for the future those in lesser status roles should benefit in terms of reward, recognition and self-worth.

If '*women as managers*' is the conventional focus of much positive action, the above suggests that some analysis and development work focused upon '*women managing at work*', usually without formal title or even self-recognition of their real role, is an equally important focus for organisations wanting to build up and value the female contribution at work. Moreover, such a focus could be a way of helping evolve management change, to foster less 'structure-bound' work organisations.

In many service organisations the manager's 'achievements' are in a fundamental sense the result of collective endeavour usually co-planned and implemented by the team or work group. In this dynamic process it is *not* given that the manager is the main planner or motivator. Many women and some men 'see' these realities in a very matter of fact way. What is equally interesting is how those with the capital 'M' for manager title are viewed by their frequently female support staff. There is a mix of protectiveness, respect and dismissiveness with a tense balance between these three attitudes usually evident. Currently in 'boss-subordinate' or 'manager-team' relationships a kind of double game occurs where there are ritualistic negotiations about who does what and who gets credit, rather than complete differences in levels and types of work. The formalities dictated by status are usually observed and they are often reinforced by the different social and work-day behaviours assumed to be appropriate for each gender. But who is actually doing which piece of work is much less neatly divided.

This does not mean that management is unnecessary but that what happens in many 'manager-subordinate' situations is much more about co-management than conventionally seen. *Management happens in a shared way*. To the extent that the manager needs, for status reasons, to be seen as the author of the plans or the prime contributor, this often happens with the consent or compliance of the 'managed'. This needs to be acknowledged, thought about and working arrangments reconsidered, — in the interests of developing both women's contribution and management approaches for the next century. For then, focus can be on developing effective work organisations from an acknowledgement of what is, rather than that which appears to be. Such development work has a double importance for women and management if female values about careers are taken into account. Women do not, in the main, hold to traditional notions of career. Studies of working women managers (see, for example, Marshall, 1984) show that whilst money is important, 'challenge and satisfaction in a particular job are more important than recurrent promotion for its own sake' (p. 23). So women's own career motivation also reinforces the need to widen the focus from developing women for a wider range of jobs to developing jobs and work organisations to take account of women's values.

In widening the focus for both positive action and organisation development we move women beyond 'Catch 22' in relation to higher status work in a way that more conventional strategies do not. The 'Catch 22' of approaches which do not include redefinition of work management is there since *either* a woman 'accepts' being disadvantaged because she is undeniably different – and by implication somewhat 'handicapped' as a potential manager – *or she* must change in order to compete on equal terms. The possibility of consciously developing management by acknowledging the shared realities of managing work is an interesting – if still largely hypothetical – way *both* to overcome this 'Catch 22' *and* to evolve new forms of workplace organisation.

Various interesting possibilities exist once such change is considered. For example, management posts and tasks could be rotated and, of course, supervisory and middle management posts reduced in number. Alongside this would be less 'status' distinctions within the workplace – surely a real drag factor in many places of employment. More fluidity in who occupies the remaining necessary formal 'Manager' posts would become normal. This could help reduce stress and burn out on the one hand and self-deprecation and cynicism on the other! Organisations' formal processes and structures could be drawn up to reflect more closely the living realities of the communications networks and co-operative endeavours which are their life blood. Organisations' charts might be drawn in a number of possible ways as shown in Figure 7.1.

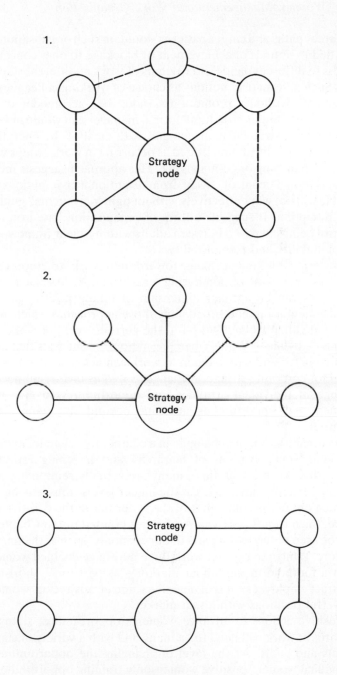

Figure 7.1

Career paths and career patterns would, in such organisations, be less tied to notions of achievement or blockage to ones concerning access to different bands and rhythms of work at different stages of life. Such 'alternative' notions as choice of working colleagues and fulfilment without promotion could be accomodated and encouraged. 'Super-structural' formal management would fade into smaller scale strategic management, with most of the operational managing openly adknowledged as occurring in work groups which are self-managing or co-managing. This approach suggests moving organisational 'control' away from traditional assumptions that people will not work effectively without tight 'patriarchial' guidance and discipline. It suggests a form of organisation based on much control being exercised between adults within a clear framework of accountability and responsibility.

Fostering this kind of change towards new work structures can be seen as one way of feminising organisations. As such, these strategies can be another dimension of taking positive action – complementary to and broadening those approaches which aim to help individual women get on in the current world of work. This chapter's byline – 'Who's Changing Whom?' – suggests that acting positively for and with women at work can acknowledge both the need for corporate structural change *as well as* the urgent need for change in individual attitudes *and* opportunities to give many women real opportunities at work beyond the female work ghettoes.

As organisations are changing in a competitive climate, many *are* shedding some symbols of hierarchy and lessening aspects of hierarchy. At the same time, many are actually reinforcing status and opportunity differences at the higher levels, thus leaving most women out in the cold – part of the lower tier in the two-tier work force. Such trends (as Lynn Ashburner pointed out in Chapter 6), can be seen in successful parts of our economy, such as the financial sector.[3] While the two tier work force may have enabled women to gain a foothold in the labour market – as part-time, short-term, contract employees – it is of negative value in 'advancing' women to powerful positions within that market.

Positive actions to advance women's opportunities, status and rewards at work will need to be many and with a variety of starting points and goals. At the level of changing the opportunities for individual women, positive women-only training opportunities are as vital as is career guidance and progressive personnel approaches to accomodate, rather than punish or exploit, the lives of working women with home-care responsibilities. The importance of networking, mentoring and, more generally, of women helping other women, is considerable, though the risks for those who reach high-status positions in being visibly pro-women remains considerable. She who is perceived to promote 'too many' other women risks her own career in some corporate circles. Perhaps the themes of individually-focused strategies can be summarised as Pioneering and Publicising, Sharing and Showing, Selling and Subverting! The role of schooling in widening girls' and young women's opportunities is also crucial, if problematic, given the gender imbalances in teaching hierarchies. Moving the hidden and overt curriculum in directions which genuinely give girls access to the whole range of subjects, particularly those relevant for careers in the technological age, remains fraught with difficulty.

Training also has a role in fostering change of attitudes and behaviours amongst managers, most of whom are men. Thus courses focused on raising awareness about attitudes towards gender and work roles have a value. They may however, like training, become ends in themselves and actually not foster changed behaviour and policy in the work place. If 'awareness training' is the major strategy of organisation and this is not followed by setting goals for change and *measuring* resultant changes, it may be an indulgence or a diversion. Nonetheless, changing male perceptions of women, particularly women in decision-making posts or in 'male stronghold' jobs, is a part of working for positive change. The power of 'outside the work place' influences is, of course, considerable in this area. The media, the family and the educational process are significant formers and reformers of men's attitudes towards women and femininity.

But the fundamental shift in women's opportunities, resources and power which is the central purpose of taking positive action also requires corporate and public change to incorporate women as equal partners in the world of work. In the 'here and now', women need survival knowledge and skills to scale man-made corporate structures. Strategies focused on developing these are a cornerstone or taking positive action. Also, in the 'here and now' of the corporate world – including the mega corporations of government – there is need to foster change in working patterns and working structures, so that women's ways of working and contributing can become part of the core of work organisations, rather than at their margins. This *is* in women's interest but it may also prove to be in the corporate interest.

How likely is it that this corporate positive action will be undertaken without complusion or overwhelming pressure? This really is an unknown, though discontent with the existing structures and patterns of work is common. In the run-up to a shift in basic patterns it is tempting to believe in the permanence of the present as a crumbling one and determination to work for a future whose form is not entirely clear. For those who wish to develop new ways of working the partnership between positive action and workplace change is likely to be powerful and productive. But as a final thought about making allowances and self-reliance, two thoughts from women of earlier times:

Man forgives women anything, save the wit to outwit him (Minna Antrim)

and

Men get opinions as boys learn to spell. By reiteration, chiefly. (Elizabeth Barrett Browning)

Notes

1. In political science literature often called 'change agents' and in the current management literature 'mono-maniacs with missions'.
2. For example, ILO Reports and Projections.
3. The trend towards creating 'fast tracks' for 'high flyers' appears to be spreading and this may reinforce women's disadvantages if entry and exit points to this track are based on masculine definitions of leadership abilities.

8

Positive action in a cold climate

RENNIE FRITCHIE

Introduction

More and more organisations within the public, private and voluntary sectors are adopting equal opportunities statements and policies. In general, such statements announce an intention to review and change organisational procedures and practices. To move from planning statements to practice is no easy task, as each chapter in this collection has demonstrated forcefully.

For those employees and managers who wish to develop or agitate for an EO change programme, this chapter contains some hints, tips and practical examples that will help develop thinking around the implementation of EO programmes. It also provides a case study of a large confectionery company that has begun to implement an EO programme. The study contains within it an account of the discussions and negotiations that took place during and after the first round of training activities within their programme's framework. The type of discussions held within the company concerning the EO issue, are not industry-specific, but commonly surface in organisations attempting to give an EO statement substance.

Whatever reason or combination of reasons those in management might have for introducing equal opportunities policies, all organisations who are seriously addressing equal opportunities issues have to be concerned with two main areas of activity. The first of these areas comprises gaining an information base on where women are located within the organisation. The second area concerns an in-depth diagnosis of the issues which affect women's career progression. The first part of this chapter sets out the steps that may be taken to address these critical areas. What follows is *not a blue print* for taking positive action, but *may be more usefully looked upon as a guide to moving forward intended or actual EO training initiatives.*

Facts and figures

Gender-based statistics and information are collated most usually for five reasons:

(a)   to discover the 'real' situation.
(b)   to find out how/why it is as it is.
(c)   to find out what people think, feel, want to be different.
(d)   to decide objectives for change.
(e)   to change/explore appropriate processes for bringing about positive change.

Having assembled key facts concerning women's employment within the organisation (for example, figures for the numbers of men and women currently employed in each grade and/or job category) the information can be used to pinpoint differences between the career progression of men and women. (For a useful guide to data gathering see 'No Barriers Here', Manpower Services Commission, 1983).

Gaining a management view

Equipped with a knowledge of the organisation as it is, it is important to gather a cross-section of management views about understanding how and why the organisation has developed so far. This is also often the beginning of raising awareness for some managers who may well be unaware of barriers to the development of women in the organisation. Through a series of individual meetings or meetings with small groups of managers, those who are recèptive to the case for pursuing EO policies can be identified. (Remember these 'warm bodies', you will almost certainly need them either to support initiatives in a hostile environment and/or to become involved directly in positive action initiatives.)

Using women's experience

A most effective way of gaining a measure of the views and experiences of women within an organisation is by affording them the opportunity to pool their experiences, aspirations and views in small groups (usually of not more than 15 in number). While it is possible to gain the views of managers on an individual basis, the views and experiences of individual women do not usually carry the same weight. Thus in order to gain a coherent organisational response to what its like being a female employee, it is strategically important that the data emerges from meetings. It can also be useful to have these meetings facilitated by someone external to the organisation.

This more general invitation has the added benefit of enabling the change agents to gauge the level of interest shown by women employees across the organisation. In meetings of one hour's duration, common themes, experiences and needs, can surface quickly. It is possible to hold five such meetings in one day! It may be desirable to follow up the preliminary meetings with a questionnaire survey of participants and to conduct some individual interviews. Using the information which results from collecting facts and figures, and adding the experiences and stated needs of women gathered through the meetings, questionnaires and interviews together with the management view, it is now possible to identify the main areas for change and prioritise them. Some likely themes are:

- traditional attitudes about women
- promotion barriers
- management style
- communication
- personnel issues
- training needs

Action areas emerge from the information gathered. Two key action areas are examined further: *recruitment* and *promotion*.

Tackling recruitment

It is important to look at how organisations find and employ people. Some organisations still recruit by word of mouth and this can perpetuate a continuance of like following like, if mainly men are working in one part of the organisation, it is likely that they will suggest others akin to themselves! If external advertisements are placed, it is important to look at both the requirement and the language. Over a period of time a job may grow and develop into something completely different. However, when the time comes to recruit for that job, a reprint of the original advertisement is often used.

The interview process itself is also important here. Men may exhibit more confidence at interview; this does not necessarily mean they will undertake the job in a more competent manner. It is important that interviewers put energy and effort into finding out the real contribution women applicants can make, rather than dismissing them because they do not 'perform' well at interview.

Looking at promotion

Many organisations have a policy to promote within if at all possible. Internal jobs may be circulated on a company memorandum. Women generally need some encouragement to apply as they have a tendency to opt out, after looking at all the requirements for the job. Women tend to dismiss themselves if they do not fulfill all the requirements perfectly. This is not usually the case with male applicants. It is worth remembering that women who have been working inside an organisation for a number of years may change their life situation; children get older (and so on). Women who are not interested in promotion previously may move towards wanting more job satisfaction and achievement of their potential. When organisations focus on the recruitment and promotion of graduates for future management positions they may overlook the rich vein of experience, dedicated women employees. A positive recent development, therefore, which some organisations are instituting are *Internal Achievers' Programmes*. These could enable a whole range of people within the organisation to begin to be considered promotable in the future, hopefully including a significant number of women.

In large organisations it is not unusual to find that employees know very little of what skills are employed and required in other departments or units. Thus in terms of women utilising the internal promotions system, it is often difficult to gain a clear idea of the requirements of the work and the kinds of processes that take place elsewhere within the organisation. It is worthwhile considering *Job Rotation* as a way of enabling women to gain wider knowledge and experience of the organisation. Temporary vacancies can be used positively, holidays, illness, or maternity leave can provide opportunities for other women. In this way women can be helped to break out of narrow departmentalism. This can also foster good working relationships across departments and divisions.

Training and *development programmes* form an important part of any positive action programme. If organisations are seriously interested in developing women, then it is likely they will consider special training programmes for women. Whilst stressing that positive action necessarily involves much more than training for women (indeed such a singular emphasis is in danger of reinforcing the idea that is women who are the problem) it must also be stressed that *such training can be an extraordinary catalyst for positive action;* bringing women together perhaps for the first time, to share and articulate experience.

Beginning training and development

Organisations who take seriously the training and development of women may consider setting up a mixed group of female and male personnel drawn from different levels from within the organisation, to take responsibility for women's development and who would report to a senior group or person. The group may be all female. This group should have the authority to suggest positive action measures within the organisation, particularly in the area of training and development.

Before starting training activities it is important to bear in mind a number of important points:

● Training programmes should be designed not only to get women on a par with men but to enable women to bring different perspectives to bear on situations. To facilitate this, training programmes should be developmental and not remedial.

Training programmes for women should be integrated into company personnel and training policies–not merely bolted on as a seperate and distinct and isolated personnel department activity.

● The organisation must review the barriers to women's development and the needs of women *with* women and to an extent with men.

● Women trainers are essential although some consider it possible to have a mix of male and female trainers.

● The training does not necessarily need to commence with a great spotlight on it. Working in quiet organic ways can be very effective.

● If the training is intended to be company-wide ¯, then it is beneficial to encourage people to attend from different parts of the organisation–in pairs, for example.

● This kind of training must be taken seriously by those providing it and those participating Both groups of people must learn to deal with snide comments like 'you women going off plotting again?' or worse!

● Look beyond the training of the organisation itself. It is all very well training women but if they want to grow and realise their potential is the organisation ready and prepared for them?

Setting the training context

Women should be allowed to choose whether or not to put themselves forward as programme participants. It can be counter-productive for managers suddenly to instruct a female employee for such a training programme. In order to ensure that accurate programme information is reaching women it is often useful to run open hour-long sessions about the why and the what of training. It is important for trainers to be available to demystify the course content method and design. Such meetings also enable trainers to hear from the women themselves about the real issues they want to raise.

It is important to consider the use of outside trainers as part of the design team, partially for credibility and expertise but also to take the 'flak' from those disbelievers in the company who are likely to be difficult. It is better that the outside person takes on the difficulties instead of the internal trainer who will have to live with company personnel long after the training. It is also important to have discussions or interviews with a range of both sympathetic and unsympathetic senior and middle managers about the barriers to women's development as well as the issues around training for women. In this way the climate in the organisation can be assessed. During discussions with managers sympathetic managers may be found and company needs which could be addressed through the training of women.

Overall course design

Course objectives should *encourage, enable* and *empower* women to develop. Continuous checking of your course design against such objectives are important.

This should include checking training materials are not written using the male personal pronoun.

It is important to be flexible in course design, to walk beside people rather than to lead them where you want to take them. It is important to leave space for *their* issues. For this reason it is a good idea to be prepared to change the course design whilst running it. (This requires considerable training expertise.)

If possible leave the timetable flexible; just giving clear headings as to the issues or subjects to be raised. In this way participants help to contribute to the course design. At the start of each day or session outline the areas intended to be covered that day and leave detailed timings out. These can be written down as the course develops. Then the trainers can spend appropriate amounts of time on the key issues.

Each course should be slightly different, even if a similar course is going to be run again and again. Trainees may wish to consider the typing up of flip charts and programmes to be sent on to people after the event.

It is important to build on current skills rather than assuming a blank sheet. In the case of women who have had considerable periods of time at home out of paid employment, helping them to identify the skills, abilities and qualities they have been using there and to see the transferability of these is vital.

Confidence building and assertiveness are liable to be important ingredients in any training for women course. It is not enough that the trainers know they can be effective, women themselves have to know it!

● Deal with the 'why women only?' issue early on, emphasising the developmental rather than the remedial approach.

Some of the most successful programmes contain four elements:

1. self diagnosis
2. skill training
3. evaluation
4. where to now?

● Follow-ups can be a great advantage. A four day course can be run in two parts–three days, then a one-day follow-up after a month, six weeks or two months.
● Encourage 'statements of intent as the completion of the first module of the course before the follow-up. *What* people intend to be working on for their own development and *how* this is going to benefit themselves and the organisation. This makes a good starting place for the follow-up and encourages people to be active in their own development in the meantime.
● Although some issues will be similar to those of men, some will be different. For example, to have a family, or not to have a family? To return to work or not to return to work after starting a family? To get the balance of home, work and leisure in some kind of order. These are key issues for women and may be increasingly so for men.
● Consider self development groups as a possibility after the follow-up module.
● Consider training of trainers; people who have attended the women's training course could become co-trainers with those from the training department in the organisation. This can help their own development and it can also help with the dissemination of courses.

Designing and developing women's training programmes is a *continuous* or *never ending* process. As with positive action in total, women's training must be viewed as a visioning for the future, and it is thus unrealistic to expect quick results.

Case study: the experience of a manufacturing company

The company employs 3000 people in the UK at 6 factories, 12 distribution depots and its Head Office site. The distribution of women employees was found to mirror the national situation: 60 per cent of the company's employees were women, 13 per cent of these were found in management positions, mostly at very junior levels. Junior and middle management vacancies were advertised internally; these vacancies were usually filled by men. Very few women applied for any management and supervisory positions. The personnel department conducted a survey of female employees to discover whether structural barriers to female promotion existed, and more specifically to pinpoint what exactly 'hampered', in a career sense, the development of women within the company. This activity was endorsed and encouraged by senior management.

A 10 per cent sample of female employees (from several different sites) was taken as the starting point for the detailed survey. The survey was conducted by the only senior female manager (responsible for office services, based at the head office), working with an external female consultant. Survey data was derived from information gained through the use of a questionnaire and follow-up semi-structured interviews with questionnaire respondents. A great deal of information concerning individual women's perceptions regarding employment opportunities, and more specifically what it felt like being a women working for the company, was amassed.

This data was used as a basis for action. An aim was to get the company to agree to running personal development workshops for women. (While positive action strategies that have a low profile may be effective in the short term, ultimately it is important if real change is to be brought about within an organisation for strategies to gain legitimacy. Thus the strategy must be sold to senior managers.) Support was sought and gained, with the proviso that similar workshops should be designed for male employees–a not unusual condition to be placed upon positive action training strategies. The workshop was presented as a unique opportunity for women from different sites and positions within the company hierarchy to help each other in their mutual development.

A pilot workshop was run for 12 women. The workshop was non-residential and included practical work on assertiveness, power, life space vs life interest and decision-making. It was successful and resulted in 8 of the original 12 wishing to become trainers on the full programme.

The next stage was to introduce and develop training skills in the 8 women who wished to become trainers. This was a very rewarding event where the new trainers overcame their natural nervousness, developed their training skills, and set about reshaping the workshop and making it their own. They took full responsibility for marketing and staffing, only requiring the help of the original trainers at their early planning meeting. Two groups were formed. One group's remit was to organise workshops exclusively for women working on production lines, whilst the other group could arrange workshops for other women in the company, Senior managers were told that all women in their departments would receive a letter outlining the aims of the workshops, when and where they would take place together with an invitation to apply. The response from women working on the factory floor was immediate, with 120 women putting themselves forward for workshops. Women who did not work on the factory floor were a little more cautious, initially; only 24 women responded. From this response 12 workshops were timetabled to run.

Further developments

Word of mouth endorsements produced further requests for places on future workshops and a growing number of women volunteered to train as trainers. The workshops were facilitated by two trainers, one from each of the two original groups, who fed back to their groups their experiences. In this way learning was shared and workshop aims remained consistent.

These workshops were run specifically to meet the personal needs of women employees but the spin-offs for the organisation have been very rewarding. Experience has shown that the women are now asking more questions, are more assertive and show more interest in their work. There is also some movement in the pattern of employment for women within the organisation. They are now applying for jobs in areas that they would not have done prior to the workshops. Some have already been promoted or are working in different jobs.

Evaluating the results and effects in this case study

In looking back at this initiative it may be of interest to set out *the company personnel directors view of developments*. In discussion it became clear that these training programmes were *very* important in making the step into action. (For even companies who pride themselves on their training can be slow to act on women's development.)

What follows are extracts from an interview by myself of the company's personnel director. We started generally reflecting about this companys' development experiences.

> *Personnel director:* We have a very concious organisation development programme for developing the culture of the organisation and individuals within it. However, on this subject of women's development I think you touch a much deeper, almost primeval instinct in individuals, particularly in men, and, although the company was able to respond, progress was only achieved by a prompting from outside the company and by the energetic efforts of some individuals from within.

Whilst such programmes can be a response to needs identified through research, they can also help identify and define those needs. The personnel director again:

> Looking back over this time, it was a turning point to find some specific activity to start in the company, and the workshops became the main example of this. They thrived. Of course, we spent a lot of time looking at women's needs, but the workshop helped them address their own needs, deepen their understanding of what they are capable of doing, and to follow some of that through after the workshop. So there was a coming together of what was needed and what was possible; there has been a tremendous response to that. We are never able to run enough workshops to meet the demand.

On the effect on women as employees:

> Women are becoming more clear about what they want and need in their lives including at work, and they are asking questions

which are not easy to respond to and answer. So it isn't easier for the company. But we are a company whose UK work force is 60 per cent female and I think what it has to gain is the potential of all its people by tapping the experience and ability and talents of all individuals.

and

On the whole women have a different way of working with people, either as a manager of people or a colleague, whatever the arrangement is. They don't work in hierarchical terms, not unless they have been conditioned by the male environment. I think there is a very interesting switch of leadership within a group where several women are present. The leading of the task actually moves fluidly according to which person has the relevant skills or experience at any particular time. There is certainly little, if any, energy wasted on politicising or vying for position. The task and process are shared.

On the next steps for the company and what else needs to be done:

Tackling the issue of moving women into what have been seen as men's jobs. Also, identifying women at all levels who are capable of and interested in doing other work, either at the same level or higher. Then helping to give them training and development they need to be strong candidates for these jobs which women have not held historically. It is essential to tie all of this in with the cultural change in the organisation and also intergrate any aims with systems. For example, we are beginning to question management development practices and how we can give people broader experience. We can ensure that any changes here automatically include women.

On the possible 'backlash' in relation to this focus on women:

When we first started the workshops we kept being told there would be backlash. However, although there have been problems and there was some backlash, it was no more difficult in dealing with the existing narrow attitudes that some individuals had anyway. We drew to the surface what was already there.

Tackling that can be a very long process, but if you accept that as part of cultural change which is in itself a long process you can actually make progress within all sorts of time scales. Do some things in one year, and others in three and others in seven or whatever, but it needs energy and it needs commitment, a core of people who can do something about it. I think it also needs women to stick with what the core are trying to do for them and with them.

Regarding successes and failures:

There are some people who more openly express their own needs and who then take the responsibility for meeting those needs. There are women who are getting to jobs that were previously male-dominated. Many areas of low pay for women have been addressed. There have not yet been any dramatic changes in the percentages of women in management. However, we are building a basis for change that will take a long time to come through intangible ways. We may not have moved a long way overall but for individuals we have and in parts of the organisation we have. The work is unstoppable now because it lives inside enough people and is not just grafted onto the organisation.

This interview perhaps gives some insights into the potential both short- and long-term of positive action training programmes for women inside 'typical' organisations.

And so ... into the future?

Unstoppable change must be the aim of a positive action programme, so that interventions mean more than a few more women in different, better places for a while. This chapter has focused very much on *'how'* to get such action underway and it has set out some specific ways of working to ensure positive action works *with* and *for* women at work. The case study interview extracts illustrate that changes in attitudes and cultures are possible if hard to 'measure'. Yet it may be these soft but pervasive changes in climate, culture and ways of working that will be the enablers of 'mass' progress for women wherever they are at work. Positive action training can work on this vision as well as the hopes of individual women to move on next month or next year to, to change the very nature of the work place; to recognise the value of women's contribution and not to deny it.

References

Acker, S. (1980) 'Women, The Other Academics', *British Journal of Sociology of Education,* vol. 1, no.1.

Acker, S., Megarry, J., Nisbet, S. and Hoyle, E. (eds) (1984) *Women and Education; World Year Book of Education 1984,* London, Kogan Page.

Adams, J. (1981) 'A Re-entry and Retainer Scheme for Career Orientated Women', *Women and Training News,* no. 5.

Anastasi, A. (1958) *Differential Psychology,* New York, Macmillan.

Arnot, M. (ed) (1985) *Race and Gender: Equal Opportunities Policies in Education,* Oxford, Pergamon/Open University.

Ashburner, L. (1986) 'Technology, the Labour Process and Gender Differentiation in the Building Society Industry's Paper to the Organisation and Control of the Labour Process 4th Annual Conference, Aston University.

Ashburner, L. Unpublished data from current research project.

Association of Cinematograph and Television Technicians (1975) *Patterns of Discriminations,* London, ACTT.

Atkins, S. (1986) 'The Sex Discrimination Act 1975: The End of a Decade', *Feminist Review,* no. 24.

Attwood, L. and McAndrew, M. (1984) 'Women at Work in the USSR' in Davidson, M. and Cooper, C. (eds) *Working Women: An International Survey,* Chichester, Wiley.

Bargh, L., Davenport, J. and Foster, J. (1986) *Developing the Insurance Industry's Womanpower,* London, Pepperell Unit, Industrial Society.

Beechey, V. and Perkins, T. (1985) 'Conceptualising Part-time Work' in Roberts, B., Finnegan, R. and Gallie, D. (eds) *New Approaches to Economic Life,* Manchester University Press.

Berger, J. (1972) *Ways of Seeing,* Harmondsworth, BBC/Penguin.

Birmingham Evening Mail (1985) 'Staffroom sexism attacked', 11 April.

Blackstone, T. and Fulton, O. (1975) 'Sex Discrimination Among University Teachers; A British–American comparison', *British Journal of Sociology,* vol. 26, no. 3.

Bradley, C. (1984) 'Sex bias in the Evaluation of Students', *British Journal of Social Psychology,* vol. 23, no. 2.

Braverman, H. (1974) *Labour and Monopoly Capitalism,* New York, Monthly Review Press.

Broad, P. (1986) *Women's Employment,* West Midlands Low Pay Unit.

Brook, E. and Davis, A. (1985) *Women, the Family and Social Work,* London, Tavistock.

Bryan, B., Dadzie, S. and Scafe, S. (1985) *The Heart of the Race; Blackwomen's Lives in Britain,* London, Virago.

Bunyan, D. and Youdale, R. (1981) *Report of a Case Study on the Impact of New Technology on Women and Trade Union Organisation in Banking,* Bristol Resource Centre.

Button, S. (1984) *Women's Committees, A Study of Gender and Local Government Policy Formulation,* University of Bristol School for Advanced Urban Studies, Working Paper 45.

Byrne, E. (1978) *Women and Education,* London, Tavistock.

Callaghan, A. (1986) Unpublished researched paper.

Chandler, C. (1986) *The Ultimate Seduction,* London, Quartet.

Child, J. (1981) *Organisation Managerial Roles: Professionals in the Corporate World,* Birmingham, Aston University.

Clwyd County Council/Equal Opportunities Commission (1983) *Equal Opportunities and the Secondary School Curriculum,* Clwyd/EOC.

Cockburn, C. (1983a) *Brothers, Male Dominance and Technological Change,* London, Pluto.

Cockburn, C. (1983b) 'Caught in the Wheels', *Marxism Today,* November.

Collinson, D. and Knights, D. (1985). 'Jobs for the Boys: Recruitment into Life Insurance Sales', *EOC Research Bulletin,* no. 9, Manchester, Equal Opportunities Commission.

Coote, A. and Campbell, B. (1982) *Sweet Freedom,* London, Picador.

Coyle, A. (1986) *Dirty Business,* Birmingham, West Midlands Low Pay Unit.

Cunningham, J. (1986) 'After the Lunacy, the Advocacy', *Guardian,* 25 November.

Daniel, W. W. (1980) 'Maternity Rights: The Experience of Women', *PSI Report,* no. 596, London, Policy Studies Institute.

Davies, C. and Rosser, J. (1985) *Equal Opportunities in the NHS,* Final Report, ESRC/DHSS Research Project, University of Warwick, Department of Sociology.

Deem, R. (1978) *Women and Schooling,* London, Routledge & Kegan Paul.

Department of Employment (1974) *Employment Gazette,* vol. 82, no.11 DOE

Department of Employment (1981) *Employment Gazette,* vol. 89, no. 4 DOE.

Department of Employment (1983) Annual Census of Employment, *Employment Gaxette,* April.

Dex, S. (1978) 'Measuring Women's Unemployment', *Social and Economic Administration,* vol. 12, no. 2.

Dex, S. (1984) 'Women's Work Histories: An Analysis of the Women and Employment Survey', *Department of Employment Research Paper,* no.33.

East Sussex Consultancy and Training Agency (ESCATA) and Institute of Local Government Studies (INLOGOV) (1985) *Managing into the Future;* a video assisted management development package for Health and Social Services, University of Birmingham INLOGOV and ESCATA.

Egan, A. (1982) 'Women in Banking: A Study in Inequality', *Industrial Relations Journal*, Autumn.

Equal Opportunities Commission (1979) *Research Bulletin*, no. 1, Winter, Manchester, EOC.

Equal Opportunities Commission (1982) *7th Annual Report*, Manchester, EOC.

Evans, J., Hills, J., Hunt, K., Meehan, E., Tusscher, T., Vogel, U. and Waylen, G. (1986) *Feminism and Political Theory*, London, Sage.

Feldberg, R. and Glenn, E. N. (1984) 'Male and Female; Jobs and Gender Models in the Sociology of Work', in Siltanen, J. and Stanworth, M. (eds) *Women in the Public Sphere*, London, Hutchinson.

Finch, J. and Rustin, M. (eds) (1986) *A Degree of Choice: Higher Education and the Right to Learn*, Harmondsworth, Penguin.

Fogarty, M., Allen, I., Allen, J. and Walters, P. (1971) *Women in Top Jobs*, London, Allen & Unwin.

Foster, M. (1985) 'A curriculum for all?' in Weiner, G. (ed) *Just a Bunch of Girls*, Milton Keynes, Open University Press.

French, J. and French, P. (1984) 'Sociolinguistics and gender divisions in Acker, S. *et al.* (eds) *Women and Education: World Year Book of Education 1984*, London, Kogan Page.

Gallagher, M. (1985a) *Employment and Positive Action for Women in Television Organisations of the EEC Member States*, Final Report, Brussels, Commission of the European Communities.

Gallagher, M. (1985b) *Employment and Positive Action for Women in Television Organisation of the EEC Member States*, Summary Report, Brussels, Commission of the European Communities.

Goldsmith, J. and Shawcross, V. (1985) *It Ain't Half Sexist Mum: Women as Overseas Students in the United Kingdom*, London, World University Service/United Kingdom Commonwealth Overseas Students Association.

Grant, R. (1984) *A Career in Teaching: Teachers' Perceptions of their Career Prospects* unpublished report, Sheffield LEA.

Grant, R. (1986) *A Career in Teaching: A Survey of Teacher's Perceptions With Particular Reference to the Careers of Women Teachers*, unpublished paper presented to the Annual Conference of the British Educational Research Association, University of Bristol.

Gregory, J. (1982) 'Some cases that never reached the Tribunal', *Feminist Review*, no. 10.

Groom, B. 'Technology is Cutting Full-Time Bank Staff', *Financial Times*, 15 April.

Hakim, C. (1979) 'Occupational Segregation', *Research Paper*, no. 9, Department of Employment, London, HMSO.

Hakim, C. (1982) *Women's Economic Activity*, paper presented to Annual Conference of the British Association for Science, Liverpool.

Handy, C. (1984) *The Future of Work*, London, Blackwell.

Harding, S. and Hintikka, M. B. (1983) *Discovering Reality*, Dordrecht, Reidel.

Henning, M. and Jardin, A. (1978) *The Managerial Woman*, New York, Anchor Press/Doubleday.

Herbert, A. (1985) 'Women in Television', in Women and Training News (eds) *Women's Training: A Ten Year Perspective,* Gloucester, Women and Training Group.

Hertzberg, F. (1968) *Work and the Nature of Men,* London, Staple Press.

Hilsum, S. and Start, K. B. (1974) *Promotion and Careers in Teaching,* Slough, National Foundation for Educational Research.

Hollway, W. (1984) 'Fitting Work: Psychological Assessment in Organisations', in Henriques, J., Hollway, W., Urwin, C., Venn, C. and Walkerdine, V. (eds) *Changing the Subject; Psychology, Social Regulation and Subjectivity,* London, Methuen.

Hoskyns, C. (1985) 'Women's Equality and the European Community', *Feminist Review,* no. 20.

Hunt, A. (1975) *Managerial Attitudes and Practices Towards Women at Work,* London, HMSO.

Hurstfield, J. (1978) *The Part-time Trap,* London, Low Pay Unit.

Inner London Education Authority (1984) *Women's Careers in Teaching: A Survey of Teachers' Views,* London, ILEA Research and Statistics.

Jenkins, M. M. and Kramarae, C. (1981) 'A Thief in the House: Women and Language', in Spender, D. (ed.) *Men's Studies Modified,* Oxford, Pergamon.

Jenkins, R. (1986) *Racism and Recruitment: Managers, Organisations and Equal Opportunity in the Labour Market,* Cambridge University Press.

Jewson, N. and Mason, D. (1986) 'Modes of Discrimination in the Recruitment Process: Formulisation, Fairness and Efficiency', in *Sociology,* vol. 20., no. 1. February.

Johnson, K. (1984) *No Room at the Top?,* London Borough of Lewisham.

Kanpinen-Toopanien, K. *et al.* (1984) 'Women at Work in Finland', in Davidson, M. and Cooper, C. (eds) *Working Women: an international survey,* Chichester, Wiley.

Kant, L. (1985) 'A Question of Judgement', in Whyte, J. *et al.* (eds) *Girl Friendly Schooling,* London, Methuen.

Keller, E. (1983) *A Feeling for the Organism,* San Francisco, Freeman.

King, R. (1978) *All Things Bright and Beautiful,* Chichester, Wiley.

Kustow, L. (1972) 'Television and Women', in Wandor, M. (ed.) (1972) *The Body Politic,* London, Stage 1.

Land, H. (1975) 'The Myth of the Male Breadwinner', *New Society,* 9 October.

Landry, C., Morley, D., Southwood, R. and Wright, P. (1985) *What a way to Run a Railroad,* London, Comedia.

Laws, J. L. (1970) 'Work Aspiration and Women: False Leads and New Starts', in Bloxall, M. and Reagan, B. (eds) *Women and the Workplace,* Chicago and London, University of Chicago Press.

Lindblom, C. E. (1965) *The Intelligence of Democracy: Decision Making Through Mutual Adjustment,* New York, Free Press.

Lindblom, C. E. (1979) 'Still Muddling, Not Yet Through', *Public Administration Review,* Nov/Dec.

Local Government Operations Research Unit (1982) *Women in Local Government, the Neglected Resource* Report no. P1. Reading, LGORU.

Local Government Operations Research Unit (1984) *Developing the Neglected Resource, An Action Report,* Report no. 2. Reading, LGORU.

London Borough of Greenwich (1986) *Equal Opportunities in Greenwich,* Internal Report, Women's Equality Unit, London, Borough of Greenwich.

Lovenduski, J. (1986) *Women and European Politics: Contemporary Feminism and Public Policy,* Brighton, Wheatsheaf.

McGregor, D. (1960) *The Human Side of Enterprise,* New York, McGraw-Hill.

Mahony, P. (1985) *Schools for the Boys?,* London, Hutchinson/ Explorations in Feminism Collective.

Malcolm, J. (1984) *In the Freud Archives,* London, Flamingo.

Manpower Services Commission (1983) *No Barriers Here,* Sheffield, MSC.

Marshall, J. (1984) *Women Managers: Travellers in a Male World,* Chichester, Wiley.

Martin, M. and Roberts, C. (1984) *Women and Employment: A Lifetime Perspective,* London, HMSO.

Maud Report, (1967) *The Committee on the Management of Local Government,* London, HMSO.

Meade-King, M. (1986) 'Why Some of the Insurance Men are Running Scared', *Guardian,* 19 November.

Meehan, E. (1985) *Women's Rights at Work,* London, Macmillan.

Merchant, C. (1982) *The Death of Nature,* London, Wildwood House.

Morgan, C., Hall, V. and Mackay, H. (1983) *The Selection of Secondary School Headteachers,* Milton Keynes, Open University.

Mouton, J. and Blake, R. R. (1978) *The New Management Grid,* Houston, Gulf Rib.

Moss Kanter, R. (1984) *The Change Masters,* London, Allen & Unwin.

Myrdal, A. and Klein, V. (1956) *Women's Two Roles,* London, Routledge & Kegan Paul.

National Union of Teachers (1984) *Primary teachers in Coventry,* Coventry Association, NUT Mimeo.

National Union of Teachers/Equal Opportunities Commission (1980) *Promotion and the Woman Teacher,* London, NUT/EOC.

Oakley, A. (1981) *Subject Women,* London, Fontana.

Payne, M. (1979) *Power and Authority and Responsibility in Social Services: Social Work in Free Teams,* London, Macmillan.

Peters, T. and Austin, N. (1985) *A Passion for Excellence,* London, Fontana.

Peters, T. and Waterman, R. H. (1982) *In Search of Excellence,* London, Harper & Row.

Peters, T. and Waterman, R. H. (1984) *The Change Masters,* London, Allen & Unwin.

Povall, M. (1984) 'Overcoming Barriers to Women's Advancement in European Organisations', *Personnel Review,* no. 13.

Povall, M., De Jong, A., Chalude, M., Racape, A. and Grozelier, A. (1982) 'Banking on Women Managers', *Management Today,* February.

Rajan, A. (1985) 'New Technology and Employment in Insurance, Banking and Building Societies; recent experience and future impact', *Special Report, Institute of Manpower Studies Series*, Aldershot, Gower.

Rendel, M. (1985) 'The Winning of the Sex Discrimination Act', in Arnot, M. (ed) *Race and Gender: Equal Opportunities Policies in Education*, Oxford, Pergamon/Open University.

Rich, A. (1979) *On Lies, Secrets and Silence*, London, Virago.

Robarts, S. (1981) *Positive Action for Women*, London, National Council for Civil Liberties.

Robbins, D. (1986) *Wanted: Railman; Report of an Investigation into Equal Opportunities for Women in British Rail*, London, HMSO.

Robinson, O. (1982) 'Part-time Labour: terms and conditions of employment', Paper presented to EOC/SSRC Conference on Part-time Work, London, City University.

Robinson, O. and Wallace, J. G. (1984) *Part-time Employment and Sex Discrimination Legislation in Great Britain*, Department of Employment Research Paper, no. 43.

Rose, H. (1986) 'Nothing Less Than half the Labs!', in Finch, J. and Rustin, M. (eds) *A Degree of Choice: Higher Education and the Right to Learn*, Harmondsworth, Penguin.

Rose, N. (1985) *The Psychology Complex*, London, Routledge & Kegan Paul.

Rowbotham, S. (1972) 'Women's Liberation and the New Politics', in Wandor, M. (ed.) *The Body Politic*, London, Stage I.

Royal Commission on the Distribution of Income and Wealth (1978) *Lower Incomes*, Report no. 6, Cmnd 7175, London, HMSO.

Ryan, M. and Medlam, S. (1984) *Blocks to Women's Career Development in Insurance*, unpublished report sponsored by the Further Education Unit (FEU).

Salaman, G. (1986) *Working*, London, Tavistock.

Sargent, L. (1981) 'New Left Women and Men: The Honeymoon is over' in Button, S. *Women's Committees: A Study of Genders and Local Government Policy Formulation*, University of Bristol School for Advanced Urban Studies, Working Paper 45.

Scott, H. (1984) *Working Your Way to the Bottom, the Feminisation of Poverty*, London, Virago.

Scott, P. (1986) 'Autonomy to Accountability', in Finch, J. and Rustin, M. (eds), op. cit.

Seebohm Report (1986) *Report of the Committee of Enquiry to Local Authority and Allied Personal Social Services*, Chairman Lord Seebohm, Cmnd 3703, London, HMSO.

Sheratt, N. (1983) 'Girls, Jobs and Glamour', in *Feminist Review*, no. 15.

Simms, M. (1985) *Women in BBC Management*, London, British Broadcasting Corporation.

Smith, R. (1976) 'Sex and Occupational Role in Fleet Street' in Leonard Barker, D. and Allen, S. (eds) (1976) *Dependence and Exploration in Work and Marriage*, London, Longman.

Snell, M. (1979) 'Equal Pay and Sex Discrimination' in *Feminist Review*, no. 1.

Spender, D. (1981) *Men's Studies Modified: The Impact of Feminism on the Academic Disciplines,* Oxford, Pergamon.

Spender, D. (1982) *Invisible Women,* London, Writers & Readers.

Stamp, P. and Robarts, S. (1986) *Positive Action Changing the Workplace for Women,* London, National Council for Civil Liberties.

Stone, M. (1984) 'Women Within Building Societies–How Do They Fare in the Industry?', *Building Society Gazette,* March.

Tarbuck, M. (1985) Unpublished report on Microelectronics in the Banking Sector.

Thames Television (1983) *Equal Opportunities in Employment,* London, Thames Television.

Thoveron, G. and Vogel-Polsky, E. (1985) *How Women are Represented in Television Programmes in the EEC,* Brussels, Commission of the European Communities.

Times Educational Supplement, (1984) 'Schooling Girls for the Dole Queue', 21 September.

Times Educational Supplement (1985) 'LEA Sex Bias Tribunal Rules', 9 August.

Times Educational Supplement (1985) 'LEA Attacked Over Bias Ruling', 25 October.

Times Educational Supplement (1986) 'NUT Survey Catalogues Sex Discrimination', 14 February.

Tolson, A. (1977) *The Limits of Masculinity,* London, Tavistock

University Statistical Record, 1982–3, vol. 1, Students or staff, USR, Cheltenham.

Vogel, J. and Zaid, L. (1984) *How Women are Represented in Television Programmes in the EEC, Part Two: positive action and strategies,* Brussels, Commission of the European Communities.

Webster, B. (1983) 'Women's Committees', in *Local Government Policy Making,* November.

Webster, B. (1985) 'A Women's Issue, The Impact of Local Authority Cuts', in *Local Government Studies,* March/April.

West, J. (1978) 'Women, Sex and Class', in Kuhn, A. and Wolpe, A. (eds) *Feminism and Materialism,* London, Routledge & Kegan Paul.

Williamson, B. (1986) 'Who has access?', in Finch, J. and Rustin, M. (eds) *A Degree of Choice: Higher Education and the Right to Learn,* Harmondsworth, Penguin.

Women's Film, Television and Video Network (1986) *Channel Four, Television and Equal Opportunities,* London, WFTVN.

Zehnder International and London Business School (1984) *Management Resources: Present Problems and Future Trends,* London Business School.

Index

190